Screen-Aware Early Childhood

A Realistic Approach to Helping Young Children Thrive in a Digitally Complex World

**Patricia Cantor, Melinda Holohan,
and Jean Rogers**

Foreword by Denisha Jones

Teachers College Press

Teachers College, Columbia University

Published by Teachers College Press,® 1234 Amsterdam Avenue, New York, NY 10027

Library of Congress Cataloging-in-Publication Data is available at loc.gov

ISBN 978-0-8077-8728-1 (paper)
ISBN 978-0-8077-8729-8 (hardcover)
ISBN 978-0-8077-8319-1 (ebook)

Printed on acid-free paper
Manufactured in the United States of America

To our children and grandchildren

Contents

Foreword

One of the many things I am grateful for is that I was born before the digital age. My generation was the last to spend hours outside engaged in free play, far from the watchful gaze or intervention of adults. Those years exploring in the woods with neighborhood kids aided my development in so many ways. I learned to trust myself, challenge my fears, stand up to bullies, protect younger kids, and negotiate time and space with others. When cellphones and Internet technology finally arrived, I was a young adult with a solid childhood grounded in physical, free play in nature, which was an important protective factor. Though I was young enough to quickly learn how to use digital devices and embrace social media, they were not a part of my core development. Unfortunately, this does not apply to children today. They are born into a world dominated by technology, social media, and screens.

As a former kindergarten teacher and early childhood professor, I am aware of the negative impacts of screen use on young children. In my kindergarten class, we had three computers, only a handful of digital games, and, fortunately, no Internet connection. Still, I was concerned about the children who chose computers every day during choice time. Their desire to spend that hour on screens every day made me question whether we should have a computer center in a classroom with 5- and 6-year-old children.

On the other hand, I remember being told that poor Black and Brown children, like the ones I taught in Washington, DC, in the early 2000s, were victims of a digital divide and needed exposure to screens and the Internet to keep up with their white, wealthy counterparts. Parents routinely made to worry because of societal disinvestment coupled with racist academic narratives targeting their children were led to believe that access to computers and screens in public schools would benefit them. So I did not get rid of the computer center. Still, I continued to be concerned that time spent playing computer games was not as beneficial as time spent in blocks, art, dramatic play, manipulatives, or the writing center.

A few years later, I was a college professor preparing future teachers and providing professional development to inservice teachers. This meant I often ventured into early childhood classrooms in public and charter schools across the district. As part of my professional development in supporting teachers to improve literacy development in preschool children, I visited a classroom that had a one-on-one tablet program. The teacher remarked how great it was that each child got to use their tablet for an hour a day. She believed the games would strengthen the literacy development we had discussed in our professional learning community sessions.

However, at 4 years old, these children had no idea how to use a tablet and were just tapping the screen to try to generate a response. The few who got a response often did not verbalize anything that would make one think they were developing phonological awareness or oral language skills. After my observation, I worked hard to support the teachers in providing child-appropriate literacy instruction without using tablets.

Unfortunately, things only got worse as I spent more time observing the growth of screens and education technology imposed on schools. And then, 2 years ago, I became a mom to two teenage children. And after finally giving in and getting them cellphones, I quickly realized how much screen time had taken over their life. I was already concerned with the time I spent on screens, but I also knew how to unplug and take a walk, practice mindfulness, or meditate throughout the day. My children, on the other hand, had to be coaxed out of their room and bribed into leaving their phones in the car. Bonding as a new family was even harder, thanks to the influence screens had on all our lives.

Fortunately, I had access to the Screen-Aware Framework for Early Childhood and other materials from Fairplay, a children's advocacy organization, that I could modify and use with my teenage children. Though my children were older, the focus on child development still applies, and it reminds me that prioritizing developmental needs is key to resisting the imposition of screens in our daily lives. As a professor of early childhood education, I appreciate how this book connects screens with the bioecological model of development and provides readers with a thorough understanding of how screens impact multiple facets of our lives. Not only do the authors disrupt screen myths, but they connect our ability to protect children through a strengths-based lens.

We cannot go back to the past and remove technology from our lives, but that does not mean we have to give up and let screens take over all aspects of early childhood. We must keep our kids *safe*, and this book is a fantastic tool to do just that.

—Denisha Jones, PhD, JD
Executive Director, Defending the Early Years

Acknowledgments

We are grateful for those whose investments contributed to birthing this book: Sarah Jubar, our editor at Teachers College Press, for approaching us at just the right time and having the insight that screen awareness is needed. The whole Teachers College Press team for their encouragement and support in developing and promoting this book. Susan Linn for her thought leadership and trailblazing advocacy. Nancy Carlsson-Paige and Diane Levin for their pioneering scholarship and generosity of spirit. Lauren Paer, Sveta Pais, and Kailan Carr for their partnership, and the Screen Time Action Network's Early Childhood Work Group members for championing the power of screen awareness. Denisha Jones, for Defending the Early Years and writing the book's foreword. Laura Teichert, for insightful review, Courtney Stevens-Kerry for design support, and Lency Ewura Esi Quainoo for research assistance. Western Michigan University's Support for Faculty Scholars Award. Fairplay, the home of the Screen Time Action Network, where we could incubate and test these concepts and practices. Our families, colleagues, teachers, and kin. And our partners in life, Al, Kevin, and Jim, for supporting and believing in us.

Introduction

As proponents of the lifelong benefits of a healthy, happy childhood, we join many others in seeking informed responses to the rapid changes in human interaction and functioning brought about by screen-based technologies and media. Our efforts focus on the urgent need to prioritize child development in a world where these technologies, and the industries behind them, hold expansive influence—with little regard for their impact on young children and the environments and relationships that nourish their growth. Our work is inspired by the hopes of families raising young children, the dedication of early childhood practitioners, and the passion of students preparing for careers in child and family services. We draw from our own personal and professional experiences and shared commitment to education and guidance that is responsive, relevant, and respectful of individual contexts and needs.

Families enjoy the benefits of screen technologies in daily life—connecting with others, capturing and celebrating their children's experiences, and accessing information and entertainment. But they also struggle to manage everyday tasks with young children, such as shopping, playtimes, and dining out, among the omnipresence of screens and the commercialized content that screens deliver. And they strive to understand and mitigate the impact of digital devices on their young children's development and behavior.

Early childhood students and practitioners express appreciation for digital technologies, especially those that enable them to access resources and create, document, and communicate effectively. At the same time, they report challenges managing screen-based content and tools while staying true to child developmental needs. And many, across a wide range of disciplines, share increasing concern about the impacts of screen use on adult-child relationships and on early learning environments, highlighting the need for developmental knowledge and informed decision-making. Common questions from those who care for and work with young children include:

- How can we understand and manage the impacts of screen technologies?

- How can we ensure that screen use is safe and manageable?
- How can we stay informed and educate others about the benefits and risks of screens?

These questions, and the strength and resilience of those raising and work-ing with children during times of rapid technological and social change, motivate and inform our work. Rooted in our Screen-Aware Framework for Early Childhood (SAFEC) and years of research, engagement, advocacy, and practice, this book offers practical information, guidance, and support for practitioners, across disciplines and experience levels, seeking to pro-mote the well-being of young children in a screen-saturated world.

NOTES FOR READERS

This book responds to the need for practical training, education, and guid-ance to support early childhood practitioners in the digital age. Screen awareness addresses the complex and changing nature of the digital land-scape, where new developments and issues continuously emerge. This book does not diminish or deny the many helpful aspects of screen technologies for caregivers and practitioners. It does recognize that the ascendency of screen-based technologies has significant implications for young children, their families, and the practices of those who serve them.

This book is specifically intended for those who care for, educate, and engage with young children from birth through age 8, the age span known as early childhood. When using the terms *early childhood, early development,* and *early learning,* we are referring to this developmental period, which is distinguished by rapid, progressive growth and maturation across physical, cognitive, social, and emotional domains. In this book, we focus on core developmental needs that children ages birth through 8 have in common, while also recognizing important developmental differences, capacities, and vulnerabilities within this 8-year span. We emphasize the research-based recommendations of the American Academy of Pediatrics for no screen time for children under 18–24 months (with the sole exception of video chat) and underscore that development in the earliest years is significantly impacted by the screen use of their caregivers. In the vignettes scattered throughout the book, we depict the effects of screen encounters on young children across the early childhood age range and consider how their care-givers use screen-aware practices, anchored in knowledge of child develop-ment, research, relationships, and protective factors, to support children's well-being.

We use the term *early childhood practitioner* to encompass the many types of professionals who work with young children and their families: infant and toddler, preschool, kindergarten, and primary-grade teachers; early interventionists; home visitors; family child care providers; administrators; early childhood instructors and trainers; teacher educators; parent educators; mental health specialists; social workers; health care professionals; children's librarians; and more.

Throughout the book, we use the terms *screens, screen media, screen technology,* and *digital media* somewhat interchangeably to refer to technology that delivers *digital media content.* This can include (but is not limited to) television, computers, smartphones, tablets, smart watches, and other devices. We also consider devices on which an actual screen isn't visible, such as virtual assistants, and some digitally enhanced toys that bring media content into children's lives.

We use the terms *parents* and *families* to refer to individuals with child-rearing responsibilities, including biological parents, grandparents, and other relatives or nonbiological caregivers. While we aim to recognize the variety of those serving in parenting roles, when describing research studies and findings we maintain the language and descriptions used in the research.

This book aims to validate your knowledge, share what we know, and present a practical, research-based framework (SAFEC) for approaching the interplay of screen technologies, screen time, and screen use as early childhood practitioners. Within these pages, you will encounter affirming and applicable support intended to help you champion the healthy development of the children and families you serve. We hope this book inspires you to nurture screen-aware relationships and environments anchored in your distinctive knowledge of the needs and well-being of young children. Together, we can shape a future that puts the developmental needs and rights of children first, ensuring that they thrive in a digital world.

CULTIVATING SCREEN AWARENESS

The current screenscape, with its opportunities and conveniences for adults, presents wide-ranging implications for child development. In Part I, we introduce the concept of screen awareness—the knowledge and practices that uphold the developmental well-being and rights of young children within a screen-based, mediacentric society. Practitioners and parents face complexities, questions, and decisions daily about children's screen exposure. We offer our Screen-Aware Framework for Early Childhood (SAFEC) as an essential guide for navigating the screenscape and making decisions about screen use. And we explore in depth the four guiding principles of SAFEC:

1. Development-centered;
2. Research-informed;
3. Protection-oriented; and
4. Relationship-based.

When used in concert, these principles provide consistent orientation for effective decision-making. We examine how protective factors—rather than risk factors—can determine children's resilience against the negative impacts of screens and help them to grow and thrive. Applying the Screen-Aware Framework introduced in Chapter 4 provides a useful tool for operationalizing SAFEC in your daily interactions and work with young children and their families.

    We expect that everyone who reads this book will bring their own perspectives on and experiences with screens and media. Yet we know we all have one goal in mind: giving children the time, space, and nurturing they need to thrive. We propose screen awareness as a viable and valuable approach to promoting children's well-being in a screen-saturated world.

At the end of each chapter in Part I you will find Questions for Reflection. We hope that these questions will challenge your thinking and help you articulate the discoveries and connections you are making as you read the book.

CHAPTER 1

Navigating the Screenscape

In this chapter, we consider the experiences of children and families amid the rapid growth of digital technologies and screen-based devices and explore the important role of early childhood professionals in providing support and guidance. We define screen awareness and examine the usefulness of viewing screen impacts through a "screen time" lens. And we introduce our Screen-Aware Framework for Early Childhood (SAFEC), a source of guidance for promoting the well-being of young children and their families in a screencentric, digitally driven world.

GROWING UP IN A SCREEN-SATURATED WORLD

When parents prepare to bring a new child into the world, they worry about planning for childbirth, establishing feeding and sleep schedules, arranging child care, and securing needed supplies—diapers, clothing, car seats, strollers—to ensure they are as ready as possible to welcome and nurture their baby. They are less likely to consider the astounding reality that the time spent developing in utero may be the only place their child will be free from exposure to screens. Their newborn will be surrounded by screen-based technologies from day one.

It can be head-spinning to think that screen-based digital infrastructures such as virtual work, commerce, education, entertainment, and social media have emerged and become commonplace within just 3 decades. This rapid transformation—termed the Great Acceleration, Digital Revolution, Information Era, and Great Rewiring, among others—has dramatically reshaped individual lives and societies within a remarkably short time period. Those growing up during the technological boom have been designated the iGeneration, eKids, Digital Natives, and 21st-Century Learners, highlighting noteworthy shifts in conceptualizations of childhood.

What does it mean to live in this digital world? Boiled down, digital is a type of electronic signal that uses a binary code, a system of numbers (digits) to transmit information. Digital signals perform far better in computer-based networks than the analog versions that preceded them, allowing for the creation of a global Internet and an explosion of devices, products, and services that utilize, organize, and distribute a vast array of digital data. Screen-based devices that deliver digital content have quickly become omnipresent across everyday environments, and the proliferation of mobile screen-based devices has all but eradicated previously screen-free spaces, generating an unceasing flow of new factors and conditions for children, parents, educators, researchers, and policymakers.

The term *screenscape* refers to the digital devices and media that people of all ages encounter as they go about their daily lives. Like landscapes or soundscapes, screenscapes can have social, cultural, and behavioral effects beyond one's control, including both consensual and nonconsensual encounters with screens. A *consensual screen encounter* is an experience with a screen-based device or screen-based media that an individual has consciously decided to activate and/or allow. Examples of consensual screen encounters include playing a game on a personal smartphone, checking a weather notification set up on a smart watch, or heading to a restaurant to watch a favorite team on a big screen with fellow fans. A *nonconsensual screen encounter* describes a screen experience that a person has little choice and/or control over (Holohan, 2024). A movie shown on an airplane that is in the line of sight but cannot be turned off, a video advertisement that runs above the gas pump when fueling, and a television playing in the center of a waiting room are some straightforward examples of nonconsensual screen encounters. Other experiences, such as activities that require using a screen-based device or opting in to screen-based content, fall somewhere between consensual and nonconsensual.

Screen-Immersed Childhoods

Despite having little to no control over their screenscapes or the ability to give informed consent to screen exposures, young children are continuously processing and responding to the screens in their environment. Consider the infant in a doctor's waiting room, repeatedly distracted by the lights and sounds of the television in the corner; the toddler in a shopping cart staring fixedly at an electronic display and screaming when it's time to move on; or the 1st-grader who persists in begging to have the in-car video system turned on during the drive to school. In these examples, children are responding to the stimulus of their screenscapes but do not have the developmental sophistication to manage their reactions or understand the impact or consequences of their screen experiences. Having not yet developed this capacity, children rely on their caregivers for help traversing the screen-based digital devices and media that they encounter. They depend on the awareness and developmental knowledge of adults to make choices that promote their well-being.

Screen media exposure—both consensual and nonconsensual—impacts children's experiences, learning, and relationships. Young children depend on the adults in their lives to manage their encounters with screens. Caregivers mitigate the impact of screens by restricting, responding, and intervening when necessary to prevent potential harm and optimize any potential benefits. As we will discuss in Chapter 5, when screen-based devices regularly distract or disrupt vital interactions with caregivers or are used to substitute for or replace relationships and activities, the likelihood of developmental vulnerabilities increases (Law et al., 2023).

Born into an attention economy driven by commercialism, young children cannot be expected to hold their own against marketing and manipulation embedded in their screenscapes. While in prior generations people needed to earn a paycheck to be considered a consumer, even very young children are now targeted because of the influence they have on family spending (Linn, 2022). Marketers seek to forge relationships with young children through products branded with media characters, advergames (addictive video games with integrated advertising), unboxing videos, and in-app ads. Social media influencers as young as 3 years old, dubbed "kidfluencers," lure young children into the world of brand loyalty and consumerism.

The advertising onslaught made possible through digital devices and media has contributed to problematic cultural trends, including age compression, the term used to describe the phenomenon of young children imitating and behaving like older children, adolescents, and even adults (Levin, 2013). For example, YouTube features 3-year-old girls recording makeup tutorials and 4-year-old boys unboxing violent video-game-themed toys. These trends indoctrinate the child influencers and their millions of followers into cultural norms that displace age-appropriate activities and encourage children to behave like teens or adults. These societal shifts in attitudes toward childhood, which we will discuss in Chapter 6, challenge traditional notions of developmental progression and raise questions about the impact of technological changes on children's identity formation, socialization processes, and well-being.

New Burdens for Families

Reflecting the changing screenscape, a Pew Research Center survey of 3,500 U.S. parents found that two-thirds believe parenting is harder today than it was 20 years ago, specifically citing digital technology and social media as reasons (Auxier et al., 2020). Surveys, interviews, and case studies consistently reveal the tensions that parents of young children experience when trying to balance the potential benefits of children's screen use with the possible harms (Findley et al., 2021; Teichert, 2017). One national survey of U.S. parents found that the majority held two apparently contradictory beliefs at the same time—that children's screen media supports their learning, but that "the less time kids spend with screen media, the better off they are" (Rideout & Robb, 2020).

Many parents believe that digital media can promote children's learning as well as support the development of digital abilities, which they regard as valuable and necessary for living in today's world. Many simply accept the presence of screens with resignation as a fixture of contemporary life, while others try to avoid screen exposure as much as possible. Parents report finding it useful to allow their young children screen time to free themselves up to accomplish household tasks or get work done, as well as to reward or attempt to regulate children's behavior. Yet parents also identify numerous concerns about the potential harms of screen use—time taken away from physical activity and outside time, interference with family time and interactions with others, exposure to harmful content, loss of privacy, and risks to health (Morawska et al., 2023).

Parents encounter conflicting information about screen use from media, health, and educational sources, from their social connections, and from tech-industry-funded professionals. And not all the information is accurate. Given diverging views about screen media usage and the conflicting information families receive, it's no surprise that many parents experience guilt, shame, judgment, and blame related to screen choices and practices.

Each family has a unique set of beliefs, values, and circumstances that influence their screen use decisions. Most parents believe they have the knowledge and capacity to determine screen guidelines for their children, and many indicate that they try to set screen-time limits. But despite their confidence in their ability to make decisions about children's screen use, parents also report feeling anxiety about the rapidly changing screenscape. They rely on trusted others—medical professionals, other parents, and educators—for guidance (Auxier et al., 2020).

The Role of Early Childhood Practitioners

Although society places inordinate responsibility on parents, the work of building screen awareness belongs to all who care for and work with young children. Early childhood practitioners play an important role. Parents of young children rank information on screen time from teachers as more influential than parenting websites, books, magazines, and social media (Auxier et al., 2020). Even more than pediatricians, who see children and parents much less frequently, early childhood professionals can build and promote screen awareness.

As an extension of reflective practice, early childhood practitioners can consider how their own values, circumstances, and experiences influence their views of digital technology and media. As an extension of culturally responsive practice, they can learn how individuals' and families' identities shape their attitudes and beliefs about screen use. And, as will be discussed in Chapter 7, they can use these understandings to approach questions and discussions about screens with sensitivity and curiosity. What practitioners know and communicate to families can be pivotal in shaping children's experiences with, and attitudes toward, screen technologies. Yet many who care deeply about young children and early learning and development find it challenging to:

- Make decisions about whether to incorporate screen-based devices and media in early childhood settings.
- Incorporate screen-based technology that is developmentally appropriate in both content and use.
- Address the varied screen media experiences, values, and needs of children and families.
- Evaluate the many messages and claims surrounding the benefits and dangers of screen use.
- Understand problematic screen technology uses, designs, and impacts, including the impacts of excessive and cumulative screen time.
- Locate reliable and actionable guidance and resources.

We hope this book will serve as a trusted guide for practitioners facing these challenges. Screen technologies can open new opportunities for innovation, discovery, and connection. They also bring new challenges for practitioners and potential harms for children, underscoring the importance of building and promoting screen awareness.

WHY SCREEN AWARE?

We define *screen awareness* as the knowledge and practices that uphold the developmental well-being and rights of young children within a screen-based, mediacentric society. Throughout this book, we present screen awareness as an emerging and essential responsibility of professionals who work with young children and their families. Screen awareness recognizes that modern childhoods intersect with a vast and expanding array of screen experiences, uses, and habits—some that promote and others that severely inhibit healthy early childhood development. Screen awareness provides an alternative to the dichotomy of fully embracing screencentric practices or avoiding screen use entirely (an option unavailable to many practitioners). Screen awareness supports informed decision-making in a complex digital world and emphasizes the importance of vigilance and advocacy when that world has not been developed with child well-being, or well-being in general, in mind.

Reconsidering "Screen Time"

A simple online search combining "screen time" and "children" unleashes a torrent of advice and opinions showcasing what has become a hot, and at times incendiary, topic for 21st-century parents, educators, researchers, and policymakers. *Screen time* refers to the total amount of time spent with any and all screen-based digital devices, often stated in terms of hours and minutes in a day. Screen-time guidelines are both widely promoted and widely critiqued. The debate is not about whether the amount of time children spend on screens matters (it does!), but how to assess, understand, and address its impacts.

Screen-time recommendations are typically the purview of health or governmental organizations seeking to positively impact public health. Built on comprehensive research analyses and consensus-building among experts, recommendations such as those from the American Academy of Pediatrics (AAP), the Canadian Paediatric Society, and the World Health Organization (WHO) are the most common type of guidance encountered by parents and practitioners. They provide specific recommendations, often organized according to developmental stages, such as the AAP recommendation of no screen time for children 18–24 months (except for video chat).

By providing clear and authoritative direction, experts aim to prevent excessive and problematic screen use. But screen-time recommendations do not always have the desired impact. Parents in the United States consistently disclose allowing more screen time than is recommended by the AAP or the WHO (Rideout & Robb, 2020). And parents worldwide indicate focusing more on the amount of time children spend on the screens than on quality of content (Dardanou et al., 2020). Parents also share that conflicting messages from a variety of sources, including variation in screen time guidance, can inflame parenting struggles and guilt (Livingstone & Blum-Ross, 2020).

Screen-time limits alone, while vitally important in the early years, are not enough to help parents to understand all the ways that screen exposure and use can affect children or to teach children the skills to successfully navigate screenscapes. Time-based advice does not address the range of potential screen harms, such as privacy violations and exposure to age-inappropriate content and advertising. It rarely considers what can be gained from screen use within family relationships and systems, such as providing a stressed caregiver a few moments for self-regulation and self-care (Barr et al., 2020; Livingstone & Blum-Ross, 2020; Nelson, 2016). As screenscapes have grown in complexity, other variables beyond time and age—such as media quality, parental media time and use, prosocial and creative media, environmental screen exposure, and displacement of nondigital activities and play—are influencing how organizations approach screen time policies and recommendations.

Digital Decision-Making

Educators, researchers, and public health experts recognize that families face growing hurdles in adhering to time-based guidance and seek methodologies better suited to the complexities and interplay of real-world conditions. The concept of the three Cs—Content, Context, Child—developed by Lisa Guernsey (2007) introduced a more nuanced framework for determining screen-time factors and effects. Guernsey emphasized that the overall impact of screen time and use also depends on the quality and developmental and educational value of the media being used (Content); the circumstances and environment in which media are used and how adults support and guide children's media experiences (Context); and the individual child's characteristics, capacities, and needs (Child).

The American Academy of Pediatrics' Center of Excellence on Social Media and Youth Mental Health, established in 2022, developed a collection of resources built on the original three Cs framework (American Academy of Pediatrics Center of Excellence, n.d.). Their Five Cs of Media Guidance—Child, Content, Calm, Crowding Out, and Communication—address "family relationships, social-emotional development, and mental health" in media guidance (American Academy of Pediatrics Center of Excellence, n.d.). Other iterations, including a variation incorporating Connections (see Blum-Ross & Livingstone, 2016), are also actively informing research and parenting strategies. A memorable vehicle for recalling and incorporating research-based considerations, this collection of "Cs," along with guiding questions related to each, serves as a helpful reference for the scope of factors involved in screen media uses, impacts, outcomes, and guidance (see Table 1.1).

THE SCREEN-AWARE FRAMEWORK FOR EARLY CHILDHOOD (SAFEC)

Navigating complex contemporary screenscapes requires tools and resources suited to the variable terrain. Created to serve as a compass rather than a road map, the Screen-Aware Framework for Early Childhood (SAFEC; pronounced "safe-see") provides dependable orientation for making decisions about screen use and meeting children's needs in the digital age (Holohan et al., 2023). Importantly, the Screen-Aware Framework for Early Childhood emphasizes that child safety—across both physical and digital environments—is the cornerstone of healthy whole-child development and the top priority of early childhood practitioners.

Table 1.1. Cs for Digital Media Decision-Making

Considerations ("Cs")	Guiding Questions
Context	• Where are digital media being used? In what settings? • How are digital media being used? Are adults present to guide media use? • For what purpose(s) are digital media being used—education? entertainment? communication? • Is digital media use balanced with other, nondigital activities?
Content	• Is the content engaging and age-appropriate? • Does the content promote interaction and learning? • Will the child be exposed to negative influences such as violence, sexualization, unrealistic body standards, or commercialism and consumerist messages? • Will the child be exposed to racially or culturally offensive influences?
Child	• Is the media content appropriate and relevant for this individual child's developmental stage? • Will this media interaction be meaningful for this particular child? • Will the content engage and build on their interests and abilities? • Will the child feel that their identity is represented?
Connections	• Will this media experience support prosocial relationships? Could it interfere with relationships? • Will it promote interaction and connection, or encourage isolation?
Calm	• Am I (or the child) using media to manage the child's emotions or stress, rather than encouraging the child to practice self-regulation?
Crowding Out	• Is media use taking the place of other activities that are beneficial for this child and family—like time with loved ones, outdoor play, physical activity, or sleep?
Communication	• Am I maintaining and encouraging open communication about media use and content? • Does the child feel comfortable bringing up and discussing concerns about media use and content?

Compiled from American Academy of Pediatrics, 2024; Barr et al., 2020; Blum-Ross & Livingstone, 2016; Guernsey, 2007; National Association for the Education of Young Children & Fred Rogers Center, 2012.

Guiding Principles

The Screen-Aware Framework for Early Childhood is based on four guiding principles for prioritizing and promoting child and family well-being across varied settings and circumstances. The guiding principles provide consistent points of orientation aligned with the knowledge and expertise of those who serve children and families (see Figure 1.1.)

Development-Centered. While the needle of a traditional compass harnesses the magnetic forces of Earth to dependably point north, the primary orientation for screen awareness is knowledge of early childhood development. Technology, educational influences, and societal pressures shift and change, but child developmental needs do not, making child development a steadfast source of guidance for understanding and decision-making. When practitioners face a choice to use screens with an individual child or in a classroom community, their knowledge of whole-child development, the needs of individual children, and group dynamics helps them determine whether use is beneficial and appropriate.

Research-Informed. Growing and substantive bodies of research serve to inform our understanding of the potential impacts of screens on children's development. Awareness of the potentially disruptive effects of screen use

Figure 1.1. Screen-Aware Framework for Early Childhood (SAFEC)

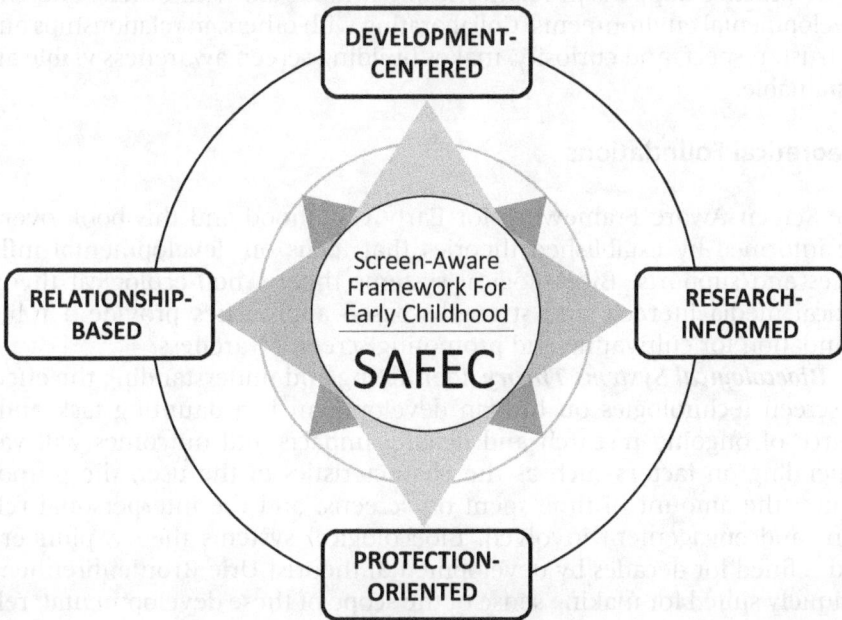

and exposure on children's physical, mental, and emotional health, learning, and growth empowers practitioners to identify and effectively implement screen-aware practices and to help children build the skills needed to
thrive in a digital world. Research provides essential guidance for identifying vulnerabilities and protective factors, implementing effective practices,
and promoting healthy outcomes.

Protection-Oriented. Protective factors are attributes that reduce the likelihood of negative outcomes or that lower a risk factor's impact. Protective
skills, priorities, and practices are grown in the home, the classroom, the program or school, the broader community, and beyond. A protective lens prioritizes child safety and supports child-centered practices, such as effectively
communicating, modeling, and setting boundaries with young children when
managing screen-based devices and media in early learning environments.
The Screen-Aware Framework promotes knowledge of protective practices
that build resilience and reduce the potential negative impacts of screen use
on children's development, learning, health, and relationships.

Relationship-Based. Screen awareness, like all early learning, is built
via relationships. Decades of research on early childhood development
establish that early learning happens best with support from responsive
adults who scaffold the child's social, emotional, physical, and sensory experiences. Screen-aware early childhood practices acknowledge the diverse
relationships, strengths, perspectives, experiences, and understandings that
children, families, and colleagues have with screen technologies. Screen-
aware practice happens in relationship with oneself, with others, and with
developmental environments. Collaborating with others, in relationships built
on trust, respect, and curiosity, makes building screen awareness viable and
sustainable.

Theoretical Foundations

The Screen-Aware Framework for Early Childhood and this book overall
are informed by established theories that focus on developmental influences and supports. Bioecological systems theory, neo-ecological theory,
critical media literacy, and strengths-based approaches provide a robust
foundation for cultivating and promoting screen awareness.

Bioecological Systems Theory. Identifying and understanding the effects
of screen technologies on human development is a daunting task and a
source of ongoing research and debate. Impacts and outcomes will vary
depending on factors such as the characteristics of the user, the purpose
of use, the amount of time spent on screens, and the interpersonal relations and engagement involved. Bioecological systems theory, pioneered
and refined for decades by developmental theorist Urie Bronfenbrenner, is
uniquely suited for making sense of the scope of these developmental, relational, and environmental variables. Bronfenbrenner originally developed

Figure 1.2. Bronfenbrenner's Bioecological Systems Theory

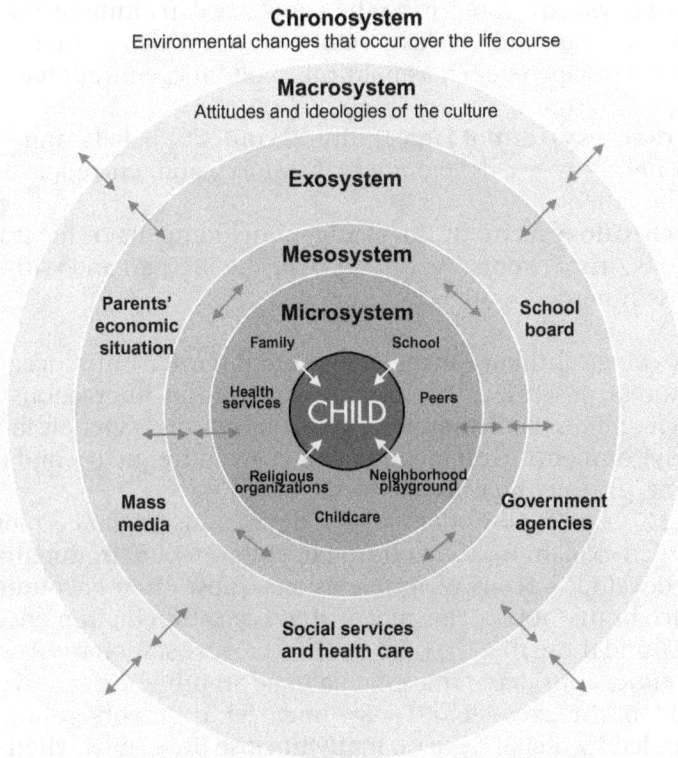

Chronosystem
Environmental changes that occur over the life course

Macrosystem
Attitudes and ideologies of the culture

Exosystem

Mesosystem

Microsystem

Parents' economic situation

School board

Family   School

Health services   Peers

CHILD

Religious organizations   Neighborhood playground

Mass media

Childcare

Government agencies

Social services and health care

this theory to enlarge the study of child development beyond what he described as "the science of the behavior of children in strange situations with strange adults" (Bronfenbrenner, 1974, p. 3). He wanted to draw more attention to the real-life settings, systems, and complex relationships that influence development rather than focusing on children's reactions to controlled experiments in lab settings with researchers.

Bioecological systems theory proposes that human development is the result of ongoing, synergistic interactions of personal characteristics (bio) and environmental (ecological) influences (Bronfenbrenner & Morris, 2006). Ecological contexts, as shown in Figure 1.2, include:

- the **microsystem**, encompassing the everyday encounters and experiences a child has in primary contexts such as home and school;

- the **mesosystem,** or the intersections of microsystems with one another and with the conditions created by the exosystem;
- the **exosystem,** comprising the people and institutions that influence the children's experiences but in which a child is not an active participant, such as political, economic, educational, and religious systems;
- the **macrosystem** of larger cultural contexts, beliefs, and values that influence the developmental context; and, encompassing all the others,
- the **chronosystem,** or the changes, including major life transitions and historical events, that occur over the lifespan and within and across systems.

As bioecological theory evolved, Bronfenbrenner introduced what he called proximal processes, the formative reciprocal interactions between the developing individual and the people, objects, and symbols in their immediate environments—interactions that grow in frequency and complexity over time (Bronfenbrenner & Morris, 2006).

In the 1970s, when Bronfenbrenner devised his original ecological systems theory to explain how everything in children's environments impacts how they develop, screens were televisions, most often encountered in a shared space in the home. This meant that typically, children encountered few screens, and those that they did encounter were stationary. At that time, Bronfenbrenner considered mass media to be an influence removed from a young child, in the exosystem. Today, however, even very young children are surrounded by digital devices, many in close proximity, whether inside or outside their primary face-to-face environments. In recognition of the powerful influence of screen technologies in the lives of children today, scholars of human development Jessica Navarro and Jonathan Tudge have proposed a new version of bioecological systems theory, which they call neo-ecological theory (Navarro & Tudge, 2022).

Neo-Ecological Theory. Neo-ecological theory adapts Bronfenbrenner's theory by identifying two types of microsystems: the physical and the virtual. Whereas Bronfenbrenner described the microsystem as the physical settings a child was likely to experience daily, Navarro and Tudge recognize that children now routinely engage in interactions and activities virtually as well as physically. Adapting Bronfenbrenner's description of the face-to-face setting of the physical microsystem, they describe the virtual microsystem as "a pattern of activities, social rules, and interpersonal relations experienced by the developing person on a given digital platform" (Navarro & Tudge, 2022, p. 19341). Virtual environments have their own sets of features that encourage or discourage engagement, just as physical environments do. It's important to note that children can simultaneously participate in interactions in both the physical and virtual microsystems, such as when a third-grader sits at her classroom desk playing Minecraft while also interacting virtually with other players in the game. An individual can even participate in more than one virtual microsystem at once—for example, a child could be simultaneously sitting in his living room, video chatting with a distant cousin on a smartphone, and using an app on a tablet.

According to neo-ecological theory, virtual microsystems have some features that are not present or are less present in physical microsystems. In virtual microsystems, activities and interactions can happen in real time (synchronously, such as in video chatting) or with a time lag (asynchronously, such as with email and social media posts). Unlike physical microsystems, virtual microsystems allow individuals not only to engage with others at a distance but also to interact with large numbers of people. These virtual interactions can be more public than interactions in the physical microsystem; for example, a social media post may reach hundreds or thousands of people, most of whom are unknown to the original poster. Virtual interactions and activities are also more likely to leave a record than physical ones. Digital photos, posts, and messages continue to exist long after their initial creation, and they can be shared and reshared with audiences far beyond those for whom they were originally intended (Navarro & Tudge, 2022).

Neo-ecological theory also places special emphasis on considering the macrosystemic influences, including cultural influences and subcultural variations, on the development of individuals in the digital age, recommending that "to understand and support today's young people, we must be prepared to examine the diverse cultures and subcultures within which they live, play, and grow" (Navarro & Tudge, 2022, p. 19345). The Internet has wrought an acceleration of cultural change, allowing new cultural (and subcultural) norms to be developed, shared, and spread rapidly and widely.

Young children today routinely interact and participate in activities in both the physical and virtual microsystems. A young child's typical day might include watching a television program while eating breakfast, listening to favorite songs on a parent's smartphone on the way to child care, doing yoga to a YouTube video in the classroom, watching ads on a screen in the grocery store checkout line, video chatting with a grandparent, playing a mobile app game with an older sibling, and falling asleep to an app-controlled sound machine. In neo-ecological theory, the mesosystem holds the interplay between a child's cumulative exposure to screen technology in various settings, parental attitudes and practices with technology, and the impact of technology on early childhood practices. The exosystem captures the impact of advertising and commercialism and the role of public policy in creating the environments in which children develop and construct meaning. Some examples might be the loose restrictions on advertising targeted at children in the United States, the rising notoriety of kidfluencers, the powerful influence of branded characters on children's preferences and desires, and the persuasive design elements built into apps, games, and ads directed at children.

Macrosystemic influences affect children's and families' access to and use of the Internet and digital technologies and include the impact of the "digital divide," or the gap between those who have the access, skills, and supports to effectively engage online and use digital tools and those who do not (National Digital Inclusion Alliance, n.d.). The chronosystem allows for consideration of the impacts of life-altering events such as the advent of social media and the global COVID-19 pandemic and the ways in which these events have transformed and influenced screen technology use and impacts across all ecological systems.

Bioecological systems theory describes the contexts and systems within which development occurs. Neo-ecological theory introduces the significant impact of digital contexts. Both theories emphasize the ways in which these contexts and systems interact and affect the developing child. The Screen-Aware Framework for Early Childhood (SAFEC) corresponds with bioecological systems theory and neo-ecological theory by providing a dynamic framework for understanding the range of relational and environmental variables that impact children's development in a screen-oriented world.

Critical Media Literacy. Educator and social justice activist Paulo Freire famously recognized that literacy must address not just the ability to read "the word" but also "the world" (Freire & Ramos, 1970). His theory of critical pedagogy championed the importance of dialogue, critical thinking, and social justice in education, challenging predominant models centered on experts who deposited or "banked" information into passive learners (Freire, 1998). Media literacy, originating in response to the rise of mass media in the mid-20th century, advances Freire's determination that education should empower individuals to question the world around them in order to actively shape their lives.

The National Association for Media Literacy Education defines *media literacy* as "the ability to access, analyze, evaluate, create, and act using all forms of communication" and describes *media* as "any medium used to transmit messages" (n.d.). In keeping with Freire's conceptualization of literacy that "reads the world," media literacy applies to analog media such as printed books, magazines, newspapers, signs, physical merchandise, and logos; digital media such as movies, podcasts, and mobile apps; and virtual media such as augmented and virtual reality experiences and computer-generated online environments. While topical subcategories and practices such as digital literacy, information literacy, and technoliteracy have emerged, overall, media literacy promotes the understanding of how media messages are constructed, disseminated, and interpreted. And, as frequently highlighted by media literacy practitioners, just as an individual would not be described as literate if they could read but not write, someone who is media-literate needs the ability to not only analyze media, but to craft and create it as well.

In an increasingly complex media culture, individuals must learn to be sophisticated consumers and creators of media. The concept of *critical media literacy* incorporates media literacy while also recognizing that "new technologies of communication are powerful tools that can liberate or dominate, manipulate or enlighten" (Share, 2015, p. 15), encouraging individuals to question, challenge, and engage with media in a socially conscious manner. The Screen-Aware Framework for Early Childhood (SAFEC) incorporates critical media literacy as both a theoretical framework and a protective factor (see Chapter 4) because critical media literacy explicitly advocates for the identification and mitigation of media dynamics and impacts—including bias, inequality, manipulation, exploitation, and power—that generate and perpetuate risks for young children, their families, and practitioners.

Screen awareness recognizes that media operate as cultural symbols, social forces, and messengers that influence children's understandings of themselves and the world. The SAFEC principles help practitioners examine rights and responsibilities in the digital age, including the power structures, business interests, and problematic digital design behind the production, distribution, and consumption of screen-based technology and media and their implications for child well-being.

Strengths-Based Approaches. The concept of strengths-based approaches comes from the fields of family support, mental health, and special education and applies across many settings and contexts. Rather than labeling children and families as "at risk" or using deficit language, strengths-based approaches rely on the central assumption that individuals, families, and communities have internal and external resources that they can draw on to promote and support their well-being (Swartz et al., 2016). These approaches focus on "what is strong, not what is wrong," on assets rather than deficits. Strengths-based practices encourage collaboration and relationship between those supported by services and those supporting them (Pattoni, 2012). Rather than swooping in as "experts" to fix problems, professionals engage with individuals and families to identify and build on their existing strengths, connections, and resources and draw on those assets to work toward positive outcomes.

Relationships that prioritize trust, mutual respect, and effective communication are the cornerstone of strengths-based approaches. Because decision-making is shared among the participants, strengths-based approaches are by nature collaborative and empowering (Pattoni, 2012, p. 2). Individuals are supported in developing the skills to independently identify goals for growth and change, as well as self-efficacy to make decisions and act. Another characteristic of strengths-based approaches is the focus on resilience, or the capacity to move forward after experiencing setbacks; this involves identifying and drawing on available resources, including connections and relationships.

In early childhood education, strengths-based approaches encourage educators to pay close attention to individual children's interests, experiences, and skills and to identify each child's unique strengths. The highly regarded early childhood education programs of Reggio Emilia in Italy are an example of a strengths-based approach in which the curriculum is informed by educators' understanding of the children's interests, ideas, and abilities, and shaped by what the children want to learn.

Many early childhood programs and services rely on strengths-based approaches to build relationships and engage with families toward the shared goal of promoting children's well-being. Advocates for strengths-based approaches regard them as beneficial for families due to their emphasis on self-efficacy, empowerment, and enhancement of social support networks (Pattoni, 2012). Strengthening Families, a strengths-based approach that focuses on helping families build protective factors that enable children and families to thrive, is well known and widely used across programs that serve young children and their families (Center for the Study of Social Policy, n.d.). The Family Protective Factors designated by Strengthening Families are particularly well suited to screen awareness, as discussed in more detail in Chapter 4.

The principles and goals of strengths-based approaches underscore the Screen-Aware Framework for Early Childhood. SAFEC promotes collaborative, engaged relationships between early childhood practitioners and families. Practitioners and families identify and use existing strengths to develop new skills for nurturing children's well-being in a screen-dependent world. Together, they work to build protective factors, or attributes that help families, practitioners, and children to mitigate the developmental vulnerabilities caused by screen time, use, and encounters and build resiliency to the ones they will encounter as they grow. The daunting challenges of navigating today's complicated screenscapes can create feelings of helplessness for practitioners and families. A strengths-based perspective offers optimism and hope.

Ever-changing screenscapes can seem chaotic and difficult to navigate, especially for adults who feel a responsibility to promote the welfare and well-being of young children. This book relieves the burden by building screen awareness—the knowledge and practices that uphold the developmental well-being and rights of young children within a screen-based, media-centric society—and providing a framework, aligned with the expertise and influence of early childhood practitioners, to orient and guide screen-aware practices. Upcoming chapters dig into the principles of the Screen-Aware Framework for Early Childhood, highlight screen-aware knowledge and priorities, and demonstrate how SAFEC can be applied across early childhood settings and circumstances. By the end of this book, you will be ready to make intentional, informed screen media decisions centered on children's healthy development; identify developmental issues related to screen use; build protective skills and knowledge; effectively communicate about screen use with colleagues and families; and promote respectful and responsive screen-aware practices and policies.

QUESTIONS FOR REFLECTION

1. What challenges or questions have families, colleagues, or friends brought to your attention related to raising and educating children in the digital age?
2. What are examples of nonconsensual screen encounters you have experienced personally and/or observed in your work with young children?
3. What is one dimension of the Screen-Aware Framework for Early Childhood that resonates with you? What is one question you have regarding SAFEC?
4. Does the neo-ecological notion that children are embedded in both physical and virtual microsystems align with your experiences? If so, how?

CHAPTER 2

Focusing on Development

Professionals who work with and care about young children and their families in any capacity understand how vital it is to have a basic understanding of child development. Any viable effort to ensure the health and happiness of children growing up in a screen-immersed society must also be informed by developmental knowledge. Early childhood educator and media producer Fred Rogers of the acclaimed *Mister Rogers' Neighborhood* television show emphasized that while "children's 'outsides' may have changed a lot over the years, their inner needs have remained very much the same." In this chapter, we highlight fundamental developmental needs in early childhood—priorities that remain constant regardless of the time, place, or pace of technological change. We share examples of how screens may support development and how they fall short, demonstrating how child developmental knowledge serves as a North Star for screen-aware decision making.

CORE DEVELOPMENTAL NEEDS

The years from birth through 8 are characterized by astonishing brain growth and amazing physical, cognitive, social, and emotional development. As they grow, young children progress through significant developmental milestones. Recognizing these milestones and the age ranges when they typically occur is useful, but early childhood practitioners must always understand that children develop at their own pace. Anyone who has spent time with a group of young children soon recognizes that even children of the same age vary significantly in terms of how they look and act. One of the authors participated for several years in a mom-and-baby group with three other mothers whose children were born within 2 days of one another in the same hospital. Although all the mothers understood intellectually that children developed at their own pace, they were still surprised by how differently this small group of babies hit their developmental milestones—one walked at 9 months, another at 18 months; one began talking at 11 months and another didn't say her first word until she was almost 3 years old and within days was speaking in full sentences. Yet all the babies were healthy, growing, and learning.

The important period of life known as "early childhood" is often divided into sub-age ranges: infants (birth to 12–18 months); toddlers (12–18 months to 3 years); preschoolers (3–5 years); and primary-grade children (5–8 years). Many child development textbooks follow this method to explore children's developmental characteristics and needs. This chapter focuses on core developmental needs that are constant across the entire age span from birth through 8, even though they may be expressed differently at different ages and stages of early development. All young children need:

- responsive interactions and connections with people who care for them;
- the support of adults to build executive function skills;
- opportunities for play and exploration;
- encouragement to experiment and try out their ideas;
- time to rest and reflect on their experiences and learning; and
- supportive environments in which to engage with others and with materials.

Knowledge of child development is central to the Screen-Aware Framework for Early Childhood (SAFEC). We encourage practitioners to consider screen and technology issues within the context of the whole child and draw from their own experiences and expertise to determine whether screens may fall short or be effective in supporting children's core developmental needs.

Human Interactions and Connections

It is impossible to overemphasize how important positive interactions with caring adults are for young children's development. Infants learn very early what it means to be part of a relationship. Infants who experience warm, responsive interactions with consistent, caring adults learn how to trust. When adults respond to a baby's body language, vocalizations, and facial expressions, infants begin to understand the pleasures of give-and-take interactions and conversations and what it means to engage meaningfully with others. Relationships are the primary way through which children learn and practice essential communication skills, both nonverbal and verbal. When caring adults take the time to learn and understand what children are trying to convey, children gain confidence and feel motivated to continue to learn to communicate ever more effectively. And when adults provide infants with physical and emotional safety and security, babies develop confidence to explore their environment, experiment with materials, and test out their emerging ideas about the world.

Stable, supportive relationships also help children build resilience to cope with challenges. Even for children experiencing difficult circumstances, the presence of just one stable, caring adult in their life can provide strong protection against negative developmental outcomes (National Scientific Council on the Developing Child, 2015). Many children have multiple caring adults with whom they develop trusting relationships. Early childhood professionals have unique knowledge of the ways positive interactions and connections benefit children's development and know how to help children develop the skills to build relationships with others.

One of the most important developmental tasks in early childhood is beginning to establish self-regulation. Self-regulation involves being able to manage one's thoughts, emotions, and behaviors. This ability is crucial not only for sustaining relationships, but for academic and eventual career success. Self-regulation takes many years to fully develop—from birth through early adulthood—and as it develops, it requires consistent, caring support from others, a process called "co-regulation" (Rosanbalm & Murray, 2017). Family members and caregivers support co-regulation by creating predictable, responsive environments and interactions. They also model self-regulation skills, such as reminding toddlers when it's appropriate to use a loud voice, demonstrating for preschoolers how to take deep breaths when they are upset, or problem-solving with first-graders to resolve a conflict over a game.

How Screens Fall Short. As described above, the relationships that help children to thrive and develop to their fullest capacity are those in which both adults and children respond eagerly to each other's cues, gestures, and language. In contrast, many interactions that young children have with screens are *one-directional* and involve predetermined scripts. For example, every time a child watches a favorite video, no matter what the child says or does, the characters in the video will behave in the same ways and say the same things. The child may feel a connection to certain characters, but that relationship will be one-sided, because the character will not be responsive to the individual child. Some programs for young children, among them *Blue's Clues* and *Ms. Rachel,* attempt to make interactions seem more individualized and responsive by having key characters ask questions of the viewer and "wait" for their response. But even in these cases, the viewer's comments or actions do not affect the character's response, which can lead to confusion and frustration for the child.

When parents or other adults give children digital devices to distract them or "quiet them down," children miss an opportunity to practice self-regulation. Although there may be occasional times when having a child watch a program or use an app frees up an adult to accomplish a necessary task or have a quiet moment to themselves, relying on digital devices to control a child's behavior can be counterproductive. Rather than learning to manage their own feelings and actions, children can become dependent on using a device to distract or occupy them. When they learn to self-regulate using internal versus external resources, children build a lifelong skill that pays dividends in the long run.

Screens and digital devices can also threaten human connections and relationships if they get in the way of or replace interactions between children and their caregivers. This type of disruption, known as *technoference*, is discussed in more depth in Chapter 5.

How Screens Can Support. Many families today rely on video chat to keep in touch with family and friends. The value of video chat for maintaining relationships was widely demonstrated during the pandemic. But even before COVID-19 hit, the American Academy of Pediatrics (AAP) identified video chat as the sole exception to its recommendation of no screen time for children under 18–24 months. AAP guidelines condone video chat episodes when they are "brief, promote social connection, and involve support from adults" (American Academy of Pediatrics Council on Communications and Media, 2016a, p. e5).

Unlike other screen media, video chat allows participants to engage with each other in real time and respond to each other's facial expressions, body language, and vocalizations or speech. Each video chat episode is unique to the individuals involved. Through video chat, for example, an out-of-town grandparent can read a bedtime story to a young child. In seeking to engage the child in the story, the grandparent may hold the book closer to the camera for the child to see details in the illustrations, ask the child questions, and respond to the child's comments and questions. The grandparent can express in words and facial expressions their delight in sharing this experience with the child and their interest in the child's reaction. This kind of responsive interaction builds connections and relationships, even across distances.

Scaffolding for Executive Function

In recent decades, researchers have recognized the important role of executive function skills in children's learning and development and the ways in which adults help children build and practice these skills in the context of supportive relationships. Executive function skills are mental processes that people use to pay attention and focus, plan, remember and follow instructions, shut out distractions, and keep several things in mind at once. Executive function skills incorporate three overlapping processes: working memory, or the ability to keep information in mind and use it as needed; inhibitory control, or the ability to exercise self-control over thoughts and actions to stay focused and follow through on a plan; and cognitive flexibility, the ability to adjust to changes (see Center on the Developing Child, 2011).

Four-year-old Maya arrives at preschool in the morning. Scanning the classroom, she sees some of her classmates playing with kinetic sand in the sensory table and notices that the sand is purple, her favorite color. Although eager to join them,

Maya first pauses to put her lunch box on the appropriate shelf and then moves her picture to the "here" basket when her teacher gently reminds her to do so. When Maya approaches the sensory table, another teacher tells her that because there are already four children there, she'll have to wait until someone leaves and asks Maya what she would like to do while waiting. Maya surveys the room again and moves to the dramatic play area.

Within the space of a few minutes, Maya has used her emerging executive function capacities to prioritize tasks, follow simple instructions, resist the impulse to run right over to the sensory table and elbow the other children aside, and adjust her priorities. Maya was not born with executive function skills. She is developing them with the support and encouragement of adults who recognize that young children are especially responsive to learning, practicing, and refining these skills (McClelland et al., 2020). Attaining and practicing executive function skills is one of the most important developmental tasks for young children. Children who have begun to develop these capacities in their early years will be able to build on and refine their executive function skills into early adulthood.

As noted in the previous section, relationships are central to children's learning and development. That is certainly the case for executive function skills. Young children are more likely to develop these capacities when adults provide consistent, predictable environments and routines and warm, responsive support by scaffolding—providing opportunities for children to practice skills with adult guidance before being able to demonstrate them on their own. In Maya's classroom, her teachers introduced consistent routines and expected the children to continue to need reminders while learning and practicing them. Routines help the children feel comfortable and confident within the setting. The teachers promote positive interactions among the children by setting some simple guidelines. These positive interactions with peers help the children develop skills they will continue to use in group settings as they move through school.

Early childhood practitioners also recognize that play, especially social play, is essential for children to develop and practice executive function skills. In play, children have many opportunities to plan, draw on working memory, exercise self-control, and adapt to changing circumstances and priorities. As children get older, games (board games, card games, song and movement games such as Red Rover and Freeze Tag) afford many opportunities to practice and refine executive function skills. As developmental theorist Lev Vygotsky observed, "In play a child always behaves beyond his average age, above his daily behavior; in play it is as though he were a head taller than himself," meaning that children can demonstrate executive function capacities more easily in play than in nonplay situations (Vygotsky, 1978).

How Screens Fall Short. Executive function skills are complex and take time to build. As noted, children develop and strengthen these skills when they receive individualized scaffolding and support from caring adults.

Maya's teacher provided scaffolding by offering reminders and asking her what she would like to do while waiting. Another child might need the teacher to be more explicit: "You'll have to do something else while you're waiting. Here are your choices . . . Which of them do you choose?" Still another of Maya's classmates might already be capable of choosing another activity without being reminded.

Screen time can have a negative effect on the development of executive function skills when it displaces activities and interactions that promote those skills: open-ended play, especially dramatic play and play with others; opportunities to use working memory, such as remembering and applying the rules of a game; and situations in which they can practice inhibitory control and self-regulation, usually with support from an adult. Most screen-based programs and apps don't require children to use these skills, reducing their opportunities to strengthen executive function. Whereas executive function skills require mental effort and concentration to develop, programs and apps are usually designed to lessen children's mental effort. Programs, apps, and even ebooks often have built-in features that distract and confuse children, causing them to have to switch attention frequently and filter out additional, extraneous information (Davis, 2023).

How Screens Can Support. A 2023 analysis of multiple research studies on screen time and executive function skills in children under age 6 identified a lack of consensus as to whether and how children's screen use impacts executive function skills (Bustamante et al., 2023). Given the complexities involved in examining this relationship, the authors concluded that more research is needed on a range of variables such as type of device, type of programming and program content, age of the child, parental involvement, and overall screen use. The researchers acknowledged that "active screen-based activities might be considered possible training to improve executive function skills," especially if the engagement occurs within a positive interaction with a caring adult, but cautioned that the effects may depend on whether the media content is age-appropriate. They reiterated the importance of play, with its accompanying emotions of joy, pride, and self-confidence, in strengthening executive function skills (Bustamante et al., 2023).

Play and Exploration

From a foundation of responsive, secure relationships with loving adults, children can venture into a rich vista of exploration and play. Through exploration and play children exercise their curiosity, discover the world around them, and make meaning out of their experiences.

Exploration and play are closely linked. This connection is reflected in the taxonomy of play developed by researcher Corinne Hutt in the 1970s. Hutt closely observed young children's play in natural settings like homes, play groups, and nursery schools. Based on her research, she identified three broad categories of playful behavior: epistemic play, ludic play, and games with rules (such as board games, card games, and active games like freeze tag).

Epistemic play, according to Hutt (1981), happens as children use their senses to investigate, examine, and become familiar with the properties of objects. The guiding question in epistemic play seems to be "What does this object do?" In *ludic play,* the guiding question changes to "What can I do with this object?," as children use what they have learned about the objects and incorporate that into pretend play, often in symbolic ways (Hutt, 1981). Exploring objects enriches children's imaginative play. For example, a child given a cardboard box might begin by picking up the box, touching all its sides, opening and closing it, putting other objects inside it and taking them out, turning it over and standing or sitting on it, even smelling and biting it (epistemic play). Then, after thoroughly exploring the box, the child might sit inside it and pretend to drive it around, or put it on his head and say, "This is my hat," or place other objects in it and pretend it's a cart full of groceries (ludic play).

Play is also intrinsically connected with learning. Developmental theorist Jean Piaget described the process of constructing knowledge as experiencing a challenge or a new situation and figuring out how to solve it (Thompson, 2017). Piaget recognized that through play with objects and with others, children realize that their actions lead to results and different actions lead to different results, helping them develop a sense of their own agency (ability to make things happen), which builds their confidence and willingness to try out their ideas.

Building on Piaget's constructivist theory, Lev Vygotsky developed the theory of social constructivism, the concept that deep learning happens through human interaction, with the help of others, and in groups (Vygotsky, 1978). He described what he called the Zone of Proximal Development, which refers to the difference between what a child can do alone and what they can accomplish with the guidance and scaffolding of supportive adults. Vygotsky also emphasized that how and what children play is strongly influenced by the individual player's experiences. All children play, but each child's play reflects their familial and cultural contexts. A child whose family owns a small store, for example, developed an elaborate dramatic play scenario in which each participant had a specific role and set of responsibilities: cashier, stocker, boss (also the mother), customers, and even "store cat."

Vygotsky regarded imaginative play as primary to children's mental health, social skills, motor skills, and executive function. Children develop compassion and empathy and learn cooperation through play. Turn-taking, planning, and problem-solving occur when children are deeply engaged in play scenarios and dramatic play. During imaginative play, children try on different roles and take different perspectives. They realize that other children can have interesting ideas that will make their play more fun. They use props to support the play: "This blanket is my cape" or "These golf balls are the meatballs I'm making." Imaginative play engages children cognitively, socially, physically, creatively, and emotionally, serving as one of the most integrative and essential activities in early childhood.

Play is notoriously challenging to define. It takes many forms—solo play, functional play, social play, sensory play, construction play, pretend play, rough-and-tumble play, nature play, and so on. Scholars of child development (of whom Hutt, Piaget, and Vygotsky are just a few) may describe play in different ways or focus on different aspects of it . All of them recognize, however, that all children have the innate desire and drive to play, and that play is essential for children's development and for deep learning to occur.

One way of thinking about play that can be particularly useful for early childhood educators is to view play as a spectrum, as described by developmental scholars and play researchers (Zosh et al., 2018). As shown in Figure 2.1, the spectrum represents a continuum in terms of who directs and initiates the experience (child or adult) and whether there is an explicit learning goal.

On one end of the spectrum is what is often referred to as "free play," play that is child-initiated, child-driven, and does not have a learning goal designated by an adult. The next benchmarks along the continuum are play experiences that the researchers describe as "guided play" and games with rules (both of which are adult-initiated and child-directed), "co-opted play" (child-initiated, but adult-directed), and "playful instruction" (adult-initiated and adult-directed). At the far end is direct instruction, which is also adult-initiated and directed but is not considered a playful experience. Except for free play, every playful experience on the spectrum has an explicit, adult-determined learning goal.

Free play affords many significant developmental benefits. Free play can be described as open-ended and unstructured, imaginative, pleasurable, intrinsically rather than extrinsically rewarding, and undertaken for its own sake rather than as a means to an end (International Play Association, 2014). Free play with open-ended materials (blocks, boxes, clay, mud, sand, water, etc.) encourages children to build on their prior ideas and creations literally and figuratively. It allows children to process their experiences, working out the feelings that arise. The more that play is directed by the child's needs, the more fully those needs are met and resolved (Levin, 2013).

Thinking about play as a spectrum provides a more nuanced view that play takes many forms, including but not limited to free play, and serves different functions. It also demonstrates that playful experiences in which children have fun and demonstrate agency can enhance their learning in classroom settings (Zosh et al., 2018). Recognizing that play benefits children's learning and development, many early childhood practitioners seek to promote "playful learning" by integrating elements of play into planned curriculum and instruction. For example, when children are playing in the pretend kitchen, a preschool teacher asks them what steps are

Figure 2.1. Play Spectrum

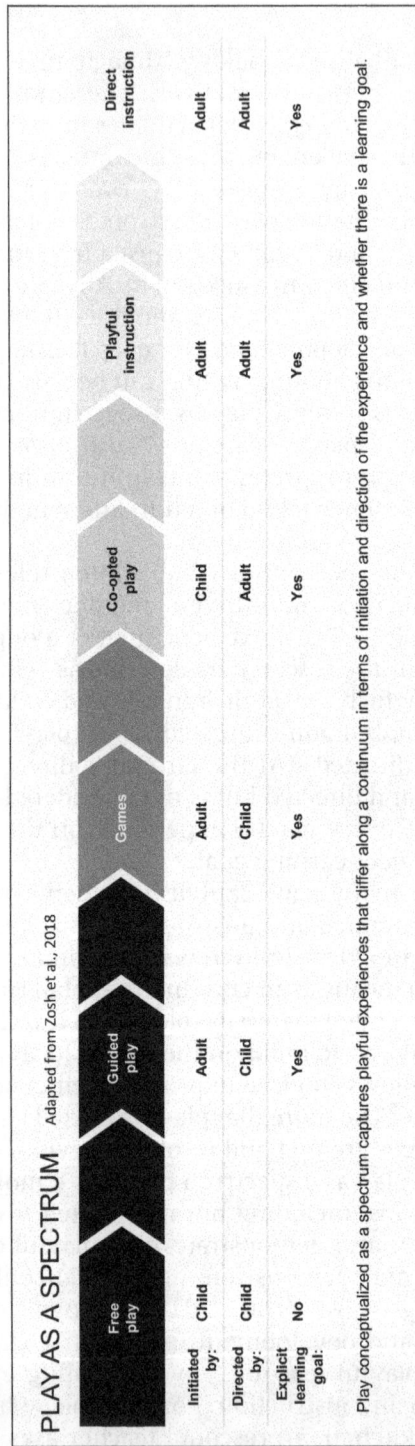

PLAY AS A SPECTRUM   Adapted from Zosh et al., 2018

	Free play	Guided play	Games	Co-opted play	Playful instruction	Direct instruction
Initiated by:	Child	Adult	Adult	Child	Adult	Adult
Directed by:	Child	Child	Child	Adult	Adult	Adult
Explicit learning goal:	No	Yes	Yes	Yes	Yes	Yes

Play conceptualized as a spectrum captures playful experiences that differ along a continuum in terms of initiation and direction of the experience and whether there is a learning goal.

needed to prepare the food before eating it. She is using guided play to lead the children toward the learning goal of sequencing. She can further emphasize sequencing by adding step-by-step illustrated recipes to the pretend kitchen. A first-grade teacher may incorporate card games, providing fun and engaging opportunities for children to practice math skills. In these examples, the teacher identifies the learning goal and designs child-directed playful experiences that children enjoy. To optimize their development and learning, children need both free play and playful learning experiences.

How Screens Fall Short. The first and most obvious way that screens fall short is *displacement,* a term used to describe how time on screens takes time away from other activities. Children who spend more time on screens spend less time in active and creative play (Yogman et al., 2018). Digital apps and games typically utilize extrinsic rewards, such as likes, stars, and streaks, robbing children of the opportunity to experience intrinsic motivation and satisfaction derived from their own explorations and problem-solving. Toys that do not have actual screens but are digitally enhanced may also discourage activity and creativity. For example, when a child turns on a switch or button to make a toy dance, sing, or do tricks, the child's role is likely to be passive. The focus is on entertainment—watching the toy go through its preprogrammed motions—rather than child-driven play.

Children's screen-based activities, whether games, apps, or videos, are often designed as targeted promotions for TV shows, movies, and other products. Playing with toys clearly identified with TV or movie characters can limit children to prescribed roles that follow the actions of the characters. When children simply copy media scripts in their play, opportunities for innovation and creativity are reduced.

How Screens Can Support. In considering how screens might support children's play, it's helpful to return to the play spectrum described in Figure 2.1. Screen activities can support playful learning when they are *intentionally designed with children's development at the forefront* and scaffolded by adults. In one example, teachers at a Reggio Emilia–inspired public preschool incorporated digital technology into their project on movies (Snider et al., 2023). After having ample time to explore digital devices and apps to learn about what the technology could do, the children drew on what they had learned to film and edit movies that they shared in the movie theater they had created in the classroom. The project itself was child-initiated and largely child-directed, with the teachers providing guidance through their intentional selection and introduction of digital tools. The project work also supported the learning goal identified by the teachers for the children to practice "academic skills like concepts of print, writing, drawing, and using data" (Snider et al., 2023, p. 27).

What About Digital Play? In the early 21st century, digital devices became an established presence in young children's lives. Researchers and educators noticed children engaging with these devices in ways that seemed similar to more traditional forms of play. These activities became referred to as digital play, a new concept still being defined and debated. Broad definitions of digital play describe it as any activities that children choose to engage with involving digital devices and toys (Plowman, 2020). Some descriptions of digital play also include situations in which children use analog objects to represent digital devices—pretending to take a selfie with a block, for example, or pretend-watching a TV program on a plastic toy (Flint & Adams, 2023).

Descriptions of digital play usually recognize that digital play involves learning to use technology while playing with it. Researchers Susan Edwards and Jo Bird created the Digital Play Framework, a digital play assessment tool to assist educators and researchers in tracking such interactions. The Digital Play Framework differentiates between epistemic and ludic digital play. In epistemic play, children explore digital devices, figure out their functions, ask adults for help in using the device, follow the directions in the device, try different actions, and develop the skills to use the device in the ways for which it was intended. In ludic play, children use the device as part of their pretend play and/or use the device in innovative ways as part of pretend play (Edwards & Bird, 2017). For example, a child might explore a digital camera by turning it on and off, snapping some photos, asking the teacher how to record a video, then recording and viewing the video he created. According to Edwards and Bird's framework, these would all be examples of epistemic play with the camera. If the child then uses the camera to record pretend play or has his peers reenact a play scene and records that, those would be examples of ludic play (Edwards & Bird, 2017).

Researchers have noted that in naturalistic settings, children's play with digital devices tends much more toward epistemic than ludic play. For example, an observational study conducted in Swedish preschools used the Digital Play Framework to collect data on 98 distinct play activities with iPads. Researchers found that the children's play with the iPads was largely epistemic. While all the children engaged in pretend play and used a variety of nondigital objects in their pretend play, there were very few instances of children using iPads as part of their pretend (ludic) play (Samuelsson et al., 2022). The researchers pointed out that their results differed from other studies that found that similarly aged children used technology in creative and innovative ways. They ascribed that difference to their observing children in naturalistic settings using widely available digital materials, rather than in lab settings using advanced technology and apps (Samuelsson et al., 2022).

Katie Davis, co-director of the University of Washington Digital Youth Lab, sounds a note of caution. While acknowledging the possibility for well-designed apps to provide some of the same developmental benefits as open-ended, child-directed play, Davis emphasizes that few such apps exist, noting that "The norm in digital play seems to be highly designed experiences that structure children's play (and attention) in specific ways" (Davis, 2023, pp. 77–78). An exception would be an app like ScratchJr, created at the

DevTech Research Group at Tufts University, that allows children to design and code their own stories and animations. But, Davis advises, "Even when designers take great pains to create virtual environments that encourage exploration and creative expression, the added layer of inflexibility associated with the digital form can limit children's range of actions more so than in the analog world" (Davis, 2023, p. 79).

Researchers agree that there is still much to learn about digital play and how it compares with nondigital play. Evolving conceptions of digital play can be confusing for practitioners seeking to implement screen awareness. The play spectrum described earlier can be useful in thinking about the potential benefits of digital play experiences for young children's development and learning, as illustrated in Figure 2.2. While it may be difficult to achieve the developmental benefits of open-ended free play when using digital devices, playful and engaging experiences incorporating digital technologies can contribute to children's learning when intentionally designed and guided by educators.

Experimentation

In 1999, researchers Alison Gopnik, Andrew Meltzoff, and Patricia Kuhl produced a seminal book on early brain development combining their expertise in cognitive science, child psychology, and speech and language development. *The Scientist in the Crib: Minds, Brains, and How Children Learn* revealed in fascinating detail the research methods used to understand the developing mind as well as the myriad ways that the exploratory activities of babies and young children mirror scientific methodology. This pioneering research on early learning and cognition opened many eyes to the relatively novel proposition that young children are the "best learners in the universe" (Gopnik et al., 1999, p. viii).

The "child as scientist" metaphor might bring to mind images of preschoolers in lab coats, or toddlers in safety goggles (which is not a bad idea!). It was meant, however, to highlight the fact that babies are naturally equipped for active, rigorous learning—a major shift from earlier views of infancy that described babies as being in a state of "blooming, buzzing confusion" or as mere "sponges" passively absorbing information. Beginning with an infant's early identification of environmental and relational stimuli and growing in skill and complexity, Gopnik et al. point out that even the youngest children "think, draw conclusions, make predictions, look for explanations, and . . . do experiments" (1999, p. viii). Notable across their summary of interdisciplinary research is the omnipresence of experimentation in early learning and cognition. One such investigation, known as the ribbon experiment, captured experimentation within the earliest stages of development. In this study, researchers tied a ribbon from one foot of each infant to a mobile hanging above their crib. They observed that infants

Figure 2.2. Digital Play in Relation to the Play Spectrum

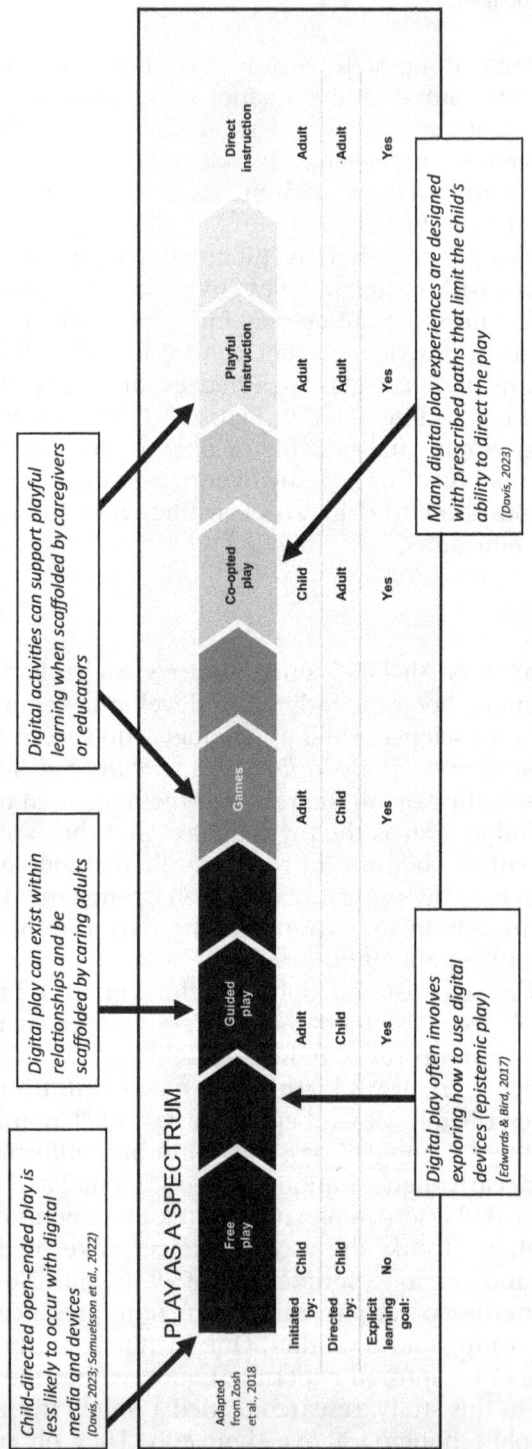

Adapted from Zosh et al., 2018

PLAY AS A SPECTRUM

	Free play	Guided play	Games	Co-opted play	Playful instruction	Direct instruction
Initiated by:	Child	Adult	Adult	Child	Adult	Adult
Directed by:	Child	Child	Child	Adult	Adult	Adult
Explicit learning goal:	No	Yes	Yes	Yes	Yes	Yes

Child-directed open-ended play is less likely to occur with digital media and devices
(Davis, 2023; Samuelsson et al., 2022)

Digital play can exist within relationships and be scaffolded by caring adults

Digital activities can support playful learning when scaffolded by caregivers or educators

Digital play often involves exploring how to use digital devices (epistemic play)
(Edwards & Bird, 2017)

Many digital play experiences are designed with prescribed paths that limit the child's ability to direct the play
(Davis, 2023)

as young as 2 months old figured out through trial and error which foot to kick to make the mobile move. Remarkably, the infants remembered this connection, kicking the same foot when they encountered the mobile again days later (Rovee-Collier & Gekoski, 1972).

Every single domain of early learning and development depends on experimentation. From an infant in the ribbon study connecting her actions to the ribbon's movement, to a toddler climbing on and touching everything in the room, to a kindergartner trying out a newly learned naughty word, experimentation is central. Through experimentation, children experience cause and effect, understand how varied actions lead to different results, and learn how to control their actions—cumulative processes that encourage them to take initiative, try out their ideas, grow confidence, establish relationships, develop competencies, and feel empowered. Ultimately, experimental processes lead to the development of identity, agency, resilience, and social responsibility—key components of successful transitions to adulthood and lifelong well-being (Scales et al., 2015).

Like good scientists, children build understanding and ability over time. When children experiment, their brains are busy processing information and making new connections (neural pathways). And, just as conventional scientific research findings must be replicated to establish credibility, children's knowledge builds through repetition and refinement.

Early childhood experimentation often involves sensory activities such as touching, tasting, smelling, observing, and manipulating different materials. These explorations activate circuits in the brain that grow sensory perception, spatial awareness, and fine- and gross-motor skills. When babies drop toys or food from a high chair, they learn that objects have different weights and compositions, make different kinds of noises, don't float upward or bounce back, and can't be recovered without someone to pick them up. When children have the chance to revisit, test, or expand a sensory experience, the developing brain retains, stores, and accesses the information more readily. As with other child developmental needs, adults play a critical role in these processes. While children may be naturally predisposed toward experimentation, their ability to do so safely, dynamically, and repeatedly depends on the engagement of their caregivers.

How Screens Fall Short. While opportunities for experimentation via screens exist, they rarely measure up to their real-world counterparts. Screens fall short when they replace (or outsource) real-world engagement, reduce multisensory experiences, fragment attention, restrict creativity, and afford limited opportunity for repetition and reflection. A screen-based painting app that allows children to make their own creations may be more open-ended than many virtual offerings, but the tools and options of the app are, ultimately, preprogrammed and finite. The child may be able to choose a large paintbrush or a small paintbrush, determine the movement of their brush, and control the selection of colors, but does not begin to have the range of variables for exploration that exist with real paints, brushes, and paper. Sensory inputs are reduced to fixed visual and sound effects. Missing are the eureka moments of discovery when the addition of one more drop of color makes the whole picture change or when a lightly applied brushstroke produces different results from a firmly planted one. The painting app user does not have the chance to smell the paint and feel its smooth texture, to ponder the drip of paint that slid down and off the paper as it dried, to experience the satisfaction of gifting the painting to a parent, or to revisit how it was made with the friend who notices it hanging on the fridge.

How Screens Can Support. When practitioners and caregivers scaffold screen use, children preschool-age and older can benefit from active use of digital devices as tools to enhance their initiatives, ideas and interests, and self-expression. When invited to document an experience via digital photography or to organize samples of their work within a digital portfolio, children experience a sense of purpose and confidence. When a child explores a variety of word-processing fonts to type a birthday message for a classmate, selects clip art images to print and cut out for a classroom activity, or engages with pre-vetted video clips that teach a new skill, concept, or perspective, screen use can be child-centered and purposeful.

Rest and Reflection

Overall, children's physical needs reveal themselves in a straightforward manner. A 5-month-old completes a series of successful attempts at rolling over, then cries in frustration at having expended the energy needed to push off his tummy one more time. A 3-year-old transforms from crabby to delightful after consuming a nourishing snack. A 6-year-old moans that her arms have stopped working after multiple attempts at mastering the monkey bars. Cause-and-effect associations between physical needs and child behaviors provide cues that help caregivers respond with a support or intervention—a power nap to counter exhaustion, a nutritious refreshment to rebuild energy, a warm bath to soothe muscle cramps and aches. The body demands respite following periods of physical exertion, and consistent interludes of rest are vital to generate and regulate energy, immune function, muscle strength, bone health, and hormones throughout childhood (Liu et al., 2024).

Periods of downtime and renewal are hugely important for the developing mind as well. When a child experiments, explores, and problem-solves, the brain is galvanized, actively growing neural pathways and generating chemicals (neurotransmitters) that support motivation and sustain interest (Caine et al., 2016). As with physical energy, mental energy is not unlimited. The brain also gets tuckered out. Intervals of restoration, during both waking and sleeping hours, provide vital balance.

The workings of the powered-down mind are central to cognitive development in young children. Neuroscientific research shows that the brain is surprisingly busy during periods of rest. Rest and sleep restore neural systems that promote brain development and enhance cognitive functions such as memory, attention, language, imagination, and problem-solving central to learning.

During rest, and particularly during sleep, the developing brain works to consolidate, sort, and store its newly acquired information and experiences—an ability known as neural plasticity—to allow for new learning (Fandakova & Hartley, 2020). While neural plasticity is present throughout life, it is most concentrated in early childhood and is reliant on periods of downtime that allow the brain to strengthen neural pathways and clear out weak and unused neural connections. Along with cultivating neural plasticity, rest helps reduce physiological stress responses in the brain that, unregulated, can impair cognitive function, learning, and memory (Brown & Jernigan, 2012).

In their daily routines, children need breaks from external stimuli and distraction as well as access to quiet time and slow-paced activity. Periods of reduced stimulus allow time and space for children to process their experiences, contemplate feedback, and expand their thinking—endeavors that promote what is referred to as higher-order learning. Higher-order learning involves actively engaging with information, making connections between ideas, and applying knowledge in new and meaningful ways. When children engage in reflective activities, such as recalling past experiences or thinking critically about new information, they activate and strengthen neural pathways, enhancing their brain's capacity to adapt and learn and advancing cognitive processes, including analysis, synthesis, and metacognition, involved in higher-order learning (Caine et al., 2016). Adults support higher-order learning by allowing children to revisit material and revise ideas over time and by modeling dispositions such as curiosity, patience, and open-mindedness. Children's cognition is also enriched when adults model cycles of inquiry—questioning, exploring, predicting, discussing, and observing—to ask open-ended questions such as "What do you think will happen?," "What did you notice?," and "What does that remind you of?" (National Center on Teaching and Learning, n.d.).

How Screens Fall Short. During waking hours, screen use takes up time that could be spent on restorative activity—coloring, looking at books, daydreaming, and being outside—and spending time on screens before naps and bedtimes can make it more difficult for children to fall asleep and stay asleep (Li et al., 2020). Many features of screen-based devices and the content distributed on them are made to capture and hold attention (see Chapter 6). Dynamic graphics, fast-paced editing, provocative sound effects, and catchy music, combined with persuasive features such as AutoPlay, gamification, and rewards, are designed to keep children engaged. But these techniques create a continuous state of stimulation that compromises developing bodies and minds.

While a child's body may appear relaxed when using an app or watching a screen, screen-delivered images, sounds, storylines, and games actually *increase* physiological and emotional arousal and reduce children's ability to pay attention (Santos et al., 2022). Unmoderated doses of stimuli from screen-based devices can overload and stress the nervous system, making it more difficult for children to relax and impairing the duration and quality of their sleep.

How Screens Can Support. When assessed for developmental appropriateness, aligned with individual capacities and temperaments, and activated for a targeted purpose, screens can support children's higher-order learning. Optimally, screen use should support a child-centered process or objective (a means, not an end), involve adult facilitation and engagement, and expand the child's experiences and thinking. The early elementary teacher who uses a reliable online information source to further a child's interest, the preschool teacher who projects an image from a book for a large-group reflection, and the parent who retrieves a digital photo to help their toddler recall a past event are each leveraging screens in ways that expand and scaffold children's understandings.

Supportive Environments

The Reggio Emilia approach to early care and education (named for its province of origin in northern Italy) is globally respected for its child-centered ideals, pedagogical emphasis on collaboration and relationships, and pioneering conceptualization of the role of the environment in children's learning and experiences (Gandini, 1993). In Reggio Emilia practice, the learning environment is explicitly identified as a "third teacher" that, in combination with the child guidance and care provided by families and educators, furnishes the contexts and conditions through which children make sense of the world around them (Biermeier, 2015). Physical environments, both natural and human-constructed, are recognized for their ability to serve as active participants in the educational process shaping and responding to children's interactions and explorations. The Reggio Emilia approach promotes responsive environments attuned to children's preferences for environmental stimuli, multisensory experiences, and social interaction. The notion of environment as an educator aligns well with the bioecological framing of human development and with research on the impacts of screen-based device exposure and use. Supportive environments also address the developmental needs described in this chapter, as follows:

- Spaces that are inviting, showcase and cultivate community, and support collaborative arrangements—child to child, child to adult, and adult to adult—help relationships thrive. Spaces that facilitate cooperative activity, play, music, and movement—a sand or water table, side-by-side easels, a large group area, or a pretend play corner—promote social connections, expressive language, and problem-solving, helping children to practice emotional regulation, conflict management, and effective communication.

- When environments are designed to support self-regulation, executive function develops more easily. Visual cues such as an illustrated daily schedule, a stop sign placed on an area that is unavailable, pictorial reminders of how many people may be at the sand table, or a step-by-step guide to setting up the snack area help children understand expectations, manage impulses, and organize themselves successfully.

- Play and exploration flourish in flexible environments that offer a variety of diverse materials stimulating imagination, language, literacy, creativity, and self-expression. Outdoor spaces encourage a wide variety of playful activities and create a sense of freedom, independence, and adventure. Outdoor environments also provide opportunities for physical challenge and risk-taking—climbing, balancing, moving large or heavy objects, and exploring new terrain—that foster self-confidence and self-efficacy.

- Experimentation thrives in settings that promote curiosity, inquiry, and hands-on investigation and allow children to access tools and materials to test their hypotheses. Environments that provide opportunities for observation, revisiting of materials and ideas, and self-assessment help refine and deepen understanding.

- Soft lighting, cozy nooks, cushions, plants, natural materials, books, puzzles, and drawing supplies invite children to slow down, relax, and engage in quiet activity. Calming spaces inspire contemplation, reflection, metacognition, higher-level thinking, and regulation of the body and mind. Environments that reduce stimulation, and that have designated spaces to decompress and recharge, support and encourage rest.

How Screens Fall Short. Features of screen-based devices such as their vivid displays and multimedia content create especially potent environmental distractions and disruptions. Young children's brains and bodies are wired for maximum receptivity to environmental stimuli, making them more prone to overstimulation and sensory overload and especially susceptible to being distracted by the *ding* of an email alert or text notification or the movement on a classroom computer screen saver. Less developed executive function makes it harder for them to tune out stimuli and maintain focus, and increases the likelihood that they will respond to distractions with lower levels of inhibition and self-control, behaviors that observant parents and educators recognize well!

How Screens Can Support. Child-centered learning environments respond to the developmental needs of each child and incorporate accommodations that ensure that children have access to the most effective and least restrictive settings, services, and supports. Screen-based technologies are used by many augmentative and alternative communication (AAC) systems to deliver tools such as speech-generated, voice output, pictorial, and symbol-based applications that serve as individualized supports for children with diverse communication abilities and challenges (American Academy of Pediatrics, 2023).

Screens can also be incorporated within early childhood environments to enrich curricular endeavors and promote connections. Monitors that showcase children's work within a community space, a projector that enlarges the content of an ongoing investigation, and devices that help children create contributions to their environment such as signs, labels, captions, or pictorial instructions are examples of screen use that supports child-centered environments and pedagogies.

QUESTIONS FOR REFLECTION

1. How have you noticed screens impacting human interactions in your life and in children's lives?
2. In your experiences with young children, what have you noticed about the influence of screen-based media characters and scenarios in their play?
3. What are your thoughts, questions, and/or concerns about digital play?
4. How have you noticed screen use affecting rest and reflection in your own life? Your friends' lives? Children's lives?

CHAPTER 3

Looking to Research

The Screen-Aware Framework for Early Childhood (SAFEC) emphasizes the importance of research-informed practices for promoting child well-being, supporting families, and avoiding unsubstantiated claims and products. In this chapter, we examine and counter common screen myths—misperceptions that arise from a lack of familiarity with the research. We summarize noteworthy research on how screen exposure and use can impair early childhood development and suggest next steps for early childhood professionals who seek to stay current and utilize research to inform their practice.

COMMON SCREEN MYTHS

Among the beliefs underlying today's screenscapes are four tenacious myths that influence the ways many people think about young children's encounters with screen-based devices and media. These pervasive misconceptions have been adopted and relentlessly promoted by profit-driven entities. Families and early childhood professionals, in their shared desire to do what's best for young children, may find themselves buying into these myths, even though the claims are not supported by research or evidence and may lead to harm.

Myth 1: The Digital Native

People who have grown up in an era of computers, cellphones, and other digital devices are often referred to as "digital natives," a term popularized in a 2001 article by education consultant Marc Prensky. Prensky claimed that digital natives think and learn differently because their brains have been transformed by their immersion in digital technology (Prensky, 2001).

Digital natives, Prensky insisted, need a faster-paced learning environment, with material presented in a less linear way. He advocated for introducing key educational concepts through short videos and by "gamifying"

after further pressure, offered cash refunds to the many families that had purchased the videos between 2004 and 2009 (Lewin, 2009).

In another case, the Federal Trade Commission (FTC) found in 2014 that the creator of Teach Your Baby to Read—a product that brought in more than $185 million—"made baseless claims about the effectiveness of the Your Baby Can Read program and misrepresented that scientific studies proved the claims" (Federal Trade Commission, 2014). A subsequent class-action lawsuit against the company led to its bankruptcy. Despite successful challenges to products that perpetuate the notion that earlier is better, the myth remains potent, and similar products continue to steadily flow into physical and virtual marketplaces.

National surveys have shown that many parents believe that their children will benefit from earlier exposure to screen-based hardware and software (Erikson Institute, 2016). They reason that because children will be expected to use tablets and computers in school and the workplace, it is to the child's advantage to have experience with touch screens, keyboards, a computer mouse, and apps as early as possible. Although advertisers heavily promote the idea that children need digital encounters to "keep up," "catch up," or "get ahead," *there is no evidence to support the perception that earlier exposure to digital media promotes school readiness.*

Aside from the concerns about the poor quality of many so-called "educational" apps, young children who don't yet have the fine motor control to manage digital devices may find these encounters frustrating and off-putting. Or they may focus on repetitive actions within a software program—such as clicking over and over on an animal to elicit a funny noise—that aren't central to the learning goals. And infants' developing brains are not equipped to process the high-intensity stimulation from screens (Children & Screens, 2024).

Myth 3: Apps Make Children Smarter

The screenscape became even more crowded in 2007, when iPhones burst onto the scene, followed quickly by iPads in 2010 and a whole range of tablets and smartphones. These digital devices made it possible to hold a computer (and the Internet) in one hand, even a small, child-sized hand. Mobile apps, software applications that could run on a handheld device, proliferated. Tens of thousands of apps, many of them labeled "educational" by their developers, were launched faster than standardized guidelines could be created. And many families downloaded and purchased these so-called educational apps and introduced their children to apps that they believed would promote learning.

The Facts. From the start of mobile apps, one of the largest and fastest-growing categories has been "educational," with thousands and thousands of apps being so designated by their makers and marketers. Many parents, searching for apps to engage their child in learning, presume that some external entity is monitoring these apps and determining whether they meet the standard of being educational. That is not the case. The term "educational" is not a protected term or determined by any agreed-upon standard, which means that app makers and advertisers do not need evidence to call their product educational.

It's no wonder that the phrase "digital Wild West" is frequently used to describe the world of apps and educational technology, including in the 2012 report *Pioneering Literacy in the Digital Wild West: Empowering Parents and Educators* (Guernsey et al., 2012). Written just a couple of years after the advent of mobile apps, the report described the "fast evolving and chaotic Wild West of digital apps" and explained that "Parents and educators face a fast-growing array of products purporting to help their children learn to read but receive little information on how or if these products live up to their claims" (Guernsey et al., 2012, p. 15). In over a decade since the report, however, little progress has been made in determining standards that apps must meet to be labeled as educational. The digital Wild West is wilder than ever.

The introduction of mobile apps also presented new opportunities for edtech companies, which quickly developed a vast array of apps for classrooms. Edtech not only promotes apps for classroom use, it also provides the devices (tablets) and even broadband to implement them (Willcott, 2017). The deluge of edtech products into schools has moved much faster than independent research could ascertain whether (or how) those products provided any actual advantages for children's learning (Escueta et al., 2020; Grose, 2024).

Employing the digital natives myth, edtech promotes the message that today's children need digitally based teaching and learning. And by exploiting the belief that "earlier is better," companies market so-called educational apps for younger and younger children.

To a parent watching a child use an app, it may appear that the child is learning. Often, the child is parroting what the app has shown them, identifying letters, numbers, colors, or shapes on the screen, or giving correct answers to simple right-or-wrong questions. The gamification of so-called educational technology—one of the ways Prensky (2001) claimed that digital natives learn—means that children's answers and scores over time are easily accessible. Just as proud parents used to hang their children's school worksheets on the refrigerator, now they are encouraged to regard children's scores in educational apps as evidence of learning. High scores on so-called educational apps can seem impressive, but the time spent is not creating sustained learning, which involves relationships, physical participation, and context (Freed, 2015). Points and rewards can motivate children to aim for higher scores, but subvert the intrinsic love of learning.

Myth 4: Parents Are Solely Responsible

Rather than being regarded as a collective social responsibility, helping children navigate screenscapes is mainly viewed in the United States as the responsibility of their parents. Since the early 1980s, when Congress dramatically loosened restrictions on television advertising and programming aimed at children, the United States has been less willing than many other nations to regulate children's media. Instead, tech companies have intentionally shaped the narrative that parents are expected to protect their children from the ill effects (Linn, 2004). It is not unusual for corporations, media, and even educational institutions to blame families for any issues associated with children's screen use, placing the burden squarely on parents to monitor and manage their children's screen encounters. Parents in turn are confused about how to teach children to navigate the screenscape. And they often feel alone and defeated in their attempts to mitigate or counteract the effects of screen media.

The Facts. The false idea that somehow parents can control *all* the ways that their children encounter and interact with screens is harmful because it fails to recognize that in the digital Wild West, a parent trying to play sheriff faces nearly insurmountable odds. Children are exposed to screens in every setting, whether or not their parents are present. Tech companies and advertisers have vast resources at their disposal and a powerful incentive to protect their multibillion-dollar profits. Advertising to parents, educators, and children is baked into nearly every online experience, using design elements that maximize engagement (see Chapter 6). Parents cannot possibly manage the impact of screens on children on their own, nor should they be expected to.

CRITICAL FINDINGS

Unlike many other consumer products, digital devices and their apps, games, and content lack regulation for safety, effectiveness, or veracity of claims before they are released to the public. Without having been proven beneficial or safe, new products continuously work their way into homes, classrooms, and other childhood environments where they impact children. But research continues to build across many important disciplines, including pediatrics, education, social sciences, and human development. For instance, well-established research on children's television viewing, an older medium, has revealed impacts on learning, play, and physical activity. These findings inform the current use of imaging systems that safely scan children's brain waves to track how engagement with screens impacts their brain activity. In children's hospitals and universities, researchers are finding distinct connections between excessive screen use and delays in development of brain areas that manage visual processing, attention, complex memory, and early reading skills (Hutton et al., 2019). Researchers are also examining the content of children's media and how that content impacts self-esteem, body image, bias, and relationships.

Since the 1990s, the American Academy of Pediatrics (AAP) has published screen-time research and guidance based on systematic review and meta-analysis of an expansive range of empirical research focused on impacts of screen time on various aspects of child development and health. The AAP recommends minimizing or eliminating media exposure, other than video chatting, for children under the age of 18–24 months and limiting screen time for children under 5 years old to no more than 1 hour per day of high-quality programming. When research findings refer to "excessive" media use, that often means more than the AAP recommendations, unless the researchers indicate otherwise.

The sections that follow present some of the significant research findings about potentially harmful effects of screen exposure and use on young children's health, development, and learning. The focus here is on negative impacts, as established across multiple research studies, because it is essential for practitioners to be aware of potential harms before making decisions about whether and how to use screen media with young children.

Physical Development

A well-established and growing body of evidence reveals that screen use has implications for the body (physical development), the heart (social and emotional development), and the mind (cognitive development) of the young child. This section chronicles the impact of excessive screen time on several aspects of physical development.

Motor Skills and Movement. Infants use their bodies to learn. By rolling, kicking, and playing with their fingers and toes, they experience themselves as physical beings in space. Screen-based products, such as tablet attachments for baby bouncy seats or child-facing device holders on strollers, restrict babies' natural inclination to move, drawing their focus to one space and reducing exploration of their own bodies and environments. When toddlers play with blocks, balls, and other loose objects, they gain muscle strength, expanded spatial awareness, and coordination skills. But when toddlers engage in excessive screen use, they are unnaturally sedentary—not lifting, stretching, or moving enough as needed for healthy development—and become at risk for cycles of weight gain, even childhood obesity, diabetes, and other ailments (Nightingale et al., 2017).

By preschool and kindergarten, children gain confidence in what their bodies can do—balance, skip, pedal, swing—which makes them eager to participate in group activities, especially outdoors. Children on a playground rarely walk from one structure to another, from the sandbox to the swings, for instance. They run! They release an incredible amount of energy and are activating positive brain chemicals responsible for decision-making, focus, and social engagement. In open-ended outdoor play, older children benefit from organizing games that involve various strength- and coordination-building elements, incorporating objects such as slides, seesaws, balls, and climbing structures (Carlson, 2011).

Even if children's screen use is developmentally appropriate, their bodies often are stationary, posing cumulative risks to physical wellness over time (Ponti, 2023). Sedentary behavior associated with screen use impacts young children's gross- and fine-motor development. Gross-motor skills, movements that require muscle coordination and strength, are required for activities like kicking, jumping, climbing, walking, and sitting. Fine-motor skills involving smaller, refined movements in the hands and wrists are required for buttoning, zipping, cutting, and writing, and for effective use of numerous tools, playthings, and implements. Both gross- and fine-motor skills facilitate the interplay between the brain and the body, making them essential components for learning and cognition.

A 2020 study of 926 children from 27 preschools found that excessive screen media use increased the risk of low gross-motor development by 72% and that inactivity in children, also associated with their screen use, increased the odds by 90% (Felix et al., 2020). Another study of preschool children over the course of 1 year revealed that greater media usage predicted worse fine-motor skills (Martzog & Suggate, 2022).

Children who spend more time with screens are shown to consume more fast foods, eat fewer fruits and vegetables, and be less physically active and fit (French et al., 2001; Robinson et al., 2017). The presence of multiple media devices during mealtimes has been shown to negatively impact the healthfulness of children's meals (Robinson et al., 2022). Reducing children's screen time results in less weight gain and obesity (Robinson et al., 2017).

Eyesight. Screens in early childhood are literally changing how children see the world. For centuries, human eyes developed to view varying distances within mostly three-dimensional settings. Features of two-dimensional screens, such as viewing angles and glare, force children's eyes to work harder, leading to eye fatigue and headaches. Excessive screen time on handheld devices is associated with a 30% higher risk of developing myopia, also referred to as nearsightedness (Yang et al., 2020). When a typical child's day includes time on multiple screens—laptops, television, tablets, and cellphones—the risk of developing nearsightedness increases to approximately 80% (Foreman et al., 2021).

In addition to the optical issues created by the screens themselves, the lure of indoor screen use can keep children from being outside, an activity proven critical to eye health. Outdoor environments provide full-spectrum bright light, a variety of spatial patterns, and sharp images of distant objects—all of which protect young eyes from myopia. Other aspects of screen use such as blue-light exposure and reduced blinking can contribute to more serious long-term vision problems (Holden et al., 2015).

Sleep. At the end of the day, deep, restful sleep helps children process their experiences. Sleep also supports healthy digestion and body growth and restores energy. While the American Academy of Pediatrics recommends no screen use (outside of video chat) until children reach 18–24 months, the reality is that many babies are now exposed from birth. For each hour of screen media exposure, an infant sleeps, on average, 13 minutes less per night (Ribner et al., 2019). In toddlers, sleep loss is attributed to blue-light exposure as well as children's active engagement with stimulating content (Mohan et al., 2021). Though this is true for all ages, the effects of blue-light exposure are even greater for young children, whose eyes are more sensitive (Hartstein et al., 2023). Sleep problems subsequently contribute to other problems, including behavior issues and obesity (Janssen et al., 2020). Screens in bedrooms not only correlate with increases in screen time but also can expose children to violent or scary content, which exacerbates sleep disturbance (Hale et al., 2018). Lack of sleep, in addition to excessive screen use, can contribute to myopia (Harrington et al., 2019).

Sensory Considerations. Screen usage isolates children's bodies from the physical world. Researchers at Drexel University College of Medicine have shown that children exposed to heavy TV viewing before their second birthday were more likely to exhibit atypical sensory processing—the body's ability to respond appropriately to stimuli received by its sensory systems. Children with too much screen time can have trouble processing what they hear, see, touch, and taste. Examples include slower responses to stimuli like their name being called or being overly upset or irritated by bright lights and noise (Heffler et al., 2024).

Social and Emotional Development

Screen overuse in early childhood removes children from critical social and emotional experiences that serve as pathways to healthy human relationships. Time on screens can take time away from key relationships pivotal to a child's sense of safety, healthy attachment, co-regulation, and self-regulation. Excessive screen use, among children and/or their caregivers, can deprive young children of the long-term benefits of essential interpersonal connections.

Attachment. When adults respond to young children's cries, babbles, and appeals for comfort, neural connections form that strengthen social and emotional development. These serve-and-return interactions shape a child's brain architecture and create a safe environment from which social and emotional intelligence can grow (Center on the Developing Child, n.d.). The Still Face Experiment, first developed in the 1970s by Edward Tronick, demonstrated the significance of the interaction between infants and parents (Tronick et al., 1978). In the experiment, mothers were asked to sit opposite their baby and not respond—keep their faces expressionless—to the infant's pleas for interaction. More recently, researchers at City University of New York (CUNY) modified the experiment, asking parents to withhold response by looking only at their cellphones.

In both Tronick's nondigital and the CUNY digital still face scenarios, infants became anxious, fearful, frustrated, and ultimately disengaged when parents stopped responding. In the CUNY study, infants also explored their toys and surroundings less, and infants of parents who self-reported greater habitual mobile device use were found to have more difficulty recovering when the parent reengaged (Myruski et al., 2018). Babies as young as two or three weeks can recognize maternal distraction. Regardless of the content, smartphone use creates a barrier to eye contact and may disrupt bonding when cell phone use is frequent (Nomkin & Gordon, 2021).

Relationships. The term *technoference* captures how digital device use can interfere with interpersonal relationships (McDaniel & Coyne, 2016). Screen use by parents during typical parent-child engagement times has been associated with fewer parent-child interactions (Radesky et al., 2014), lower responsiveness to child bids for attention (Hinkley et al., 2014), and even hostility from the parent toward the children's bids. Both children and parents report discomfort with parental technology use. "Absent presence," or parents being physically in the same space but distracted by a device during family daily routines, had similar outcomes (McDaniel & Radesky, 2017).

The term *technovoidance* suggests using technology to avoid unpleasant emotions, tasks, and interpersonal interactions (Browne, 2018). Adults might scroll through social media to avoid chores or binge-watch favorite programs to decompress after a stressful day at work. Children may be handed devices because they are tired, fussy, or agitated. While the device may appear to calm them, it deprives them of the opportunity to learn how to self-soothe and self-regulate—skills essential for stress and behavior management—via the comfort and co-regulation provided by caregivers. Behavior problems can ensue.

Young children's healthy development depends upon caring, responsive relationships with others. Caregiver-child connections are so essential that we have devoted an entire chapter (Chapter 5) to strategies for fortifying those relationships. Both technoference and technovoidance have negative implications for adult-child relationships that are also explored in Chapter 5.

Cognitive Development

Children's brains grow rapidly and extensively during their early years, and so do their cognitive abilities to think, reason, make meaning, and problem-solve. As with other aspects of whole-child development, screen use can have significant impacts on children's cognitive development, including attention, communication and language skills, and reading skills.

Attention and Executive Function. One nonconsensual screen encounter, "background TV," remains a common experience for children under 8 (Rideout & Robb, 2020). Background TV happens when the television is on while a child is engaged in other activities such as playing, eating, or interacting with others (Anderson & Hanson, 2013). Despite the popularity of new media, television is still a major presence in many young children's lives. According to a 2020 survey conducted by Common Sense Media, the TV was on for all or most of the day in 39% of homes of children under age 8 (Rideout & Robb, 2020, p. 22).

Background television significantly impacts young children's attention. Even when the program is of no interest to a young child—such as a sporting event or a show targeted to adults—background TV is distracting to both children and adults and has negative associations for children's language development, attention, and play. Researchers speculate that the sounds and visual effects of the background TV compete for children's attention, pulling them away from their activities, even if they don't understand what the program is about (Barr et al., 2018). Over time, this distraction negatively affects children's ability to sustain focus and attention.

Researchers have found that frequent exposure to background TV was associated with reduced attention and lower verbal IQ, as well as delays in language and cognitive development (Anderson & Hanson, 2013; Martinot et al., 2021). While child-directed background TV programming is more likely to pull preschoolers away from their play and hold their attention, adult-directed programming is also disruptive (O'Toole & Kannass, 2021).

A 2021 survey of 1,180 caregivers of children aged 2–8 in the United States explored links between background television exposure and executive function skills. Based on caregiver reporting, the preschoolers experienced 4.1 hours of background television daily, and school-age children 2.8 hours. The researchers found that having the TV on in the background during sleep predicted poorer executive function skills for all children, and background TV had a negative impact on executive function skills for preschoolers playing by themselves. The authors expressed concern about the long-term impact of background TV exposure on executive function skills and affirmed their support of the American Academy of Pediatrics' recommendation to turn off background TV when children are present (Nichols, 2022, p. 1173).

Communication and Language Skills. Interactive conversations are the "golden nugget" of child development, according to Kathy Hirsh-Pasek, director of the Infant Language Laboratory at Temple University. "Having fluid, interactive conversations really helps a child learn language," she explains, "and language is the single-best predictor of everything academic that's going to come their way" (quoted in Puglisi, n.d.). Children learn language and increase their communication skills by hearing words in context, in social settings, so that they can make meaning from them. Children ages 2½ to 3 years and up can learn vocabulary and other skills and concepts from screen media, but infants and toddlers do not learn from screen programming and require in-person interactions and exchanges (Barr et al., 2018). Researchers have coined the term *transfer deficit* (also known as video deficit effect) to describe this phenomenon. Transfer deficit occurs across many types of tasks on screen devices (TV, smartphones, tablets).

Consider, for example, how a young child learns what "hot" means. As an infant, she hears adults and older siblings using the word "hot" and experiences "hot" in various ways—the weather is hot, the steam she sees rising from the coffee is hot, the slide on the playground is hot, touching the radiator is hot, the sun feels hot. After repeatedly hearing and experiencing the word "hot" used in these contexts, the child will begin saying "hot" when she sees steam rising from a pot on the stove or when she feels the heat on her skin. Her family members and teachers will confirm, "yes, that's hot! Hot!," and her understanding will grow. Compare that to seeing a picture of a fire or a cup of coffee and being told that that is "hot." The picture can't convey the physical sensations of "hot," which makes it difficult for a very young child to fully understand the concept.

In video chat, very young children depend strongly on the social cues of co-viewers to make sense of the experience. Some studies indicate that older toddlers may be able to learn new vocabulary through video chat if it is live and socially contingent, meaning that adults in the chat are responsive to the toddler's cues (Davis, 2023). Proximal reciprocity with a physically present adult contributed to toddler engagement with video chat, and toddlers looked to their co-viewer during video chat more often and remained engaged longer when their co-viewer was responsive, versus unresponsive (Myers et al., 2018). This research reinforces the understanding that infants and toddlers learn most effectively through responsive, contingent, individualized real-life interactions.

Numerous studies reveal that more screen time equates to smaller vocabularies and delayed expressive language skills compared to children with less or no exposure to screens. A recent 4-year study in Japan of over 7,000 mother/child pairs found that children who were exposed to more screen time at age 1 were more likely to have delays in communication and problem-solving skills at ages 2 and 4 (Takahashi et al., 2023). Background television also impacts young children's language. They are less likely to vocalize and engage in conversation with caregivers and siblings when the TV is on.

A notable 2009 study found that the more infants and toddlers were exposed to television, the less language they produced (Christakis et al., 2009). The same study noted that adults tend to talk less with children when the television is on, reducing the opportunities for conversational interactions and exchanges that are essential for language development (Christakis et al., 2009).

Many parents believe advertisers' claims that certain television programs or apps can enhance their children's language development, learning, and cognition (Karani et al., 2022). Unfortunately, increased viewing time may have the opposite effect of what well-meaning parents intend. A 2022 review of multiple studies from several countries on the impact of screen time on children's language development found that children with an earlier age of onset for screen exposure and greater screen time, particularly before age 2, were more likely to experience negative effects on language development. Although an older age of onset of screen viewing was associated with some benefits, overall "it appears that the negative influences outweigh the positive influences" (Karani et al., 2022, p. 6). As noted, researcher and doctor Dimitri Christakis emphasizes, "there is no evidence that children acquire anything meaningful from screens before the age of 18 months . . . Simply put, young children need laps, not apps" (Children & Screens, 2024).

An analysis of over 40 studies focused on child language and screen use found that for children preschool-age and older, educational programming may be associated with increased language skills; however, it can be difficult to identify the type of programming most likely to promote language development. The authors state that "It is important to note that the quality of educational programs varied from study to study and therefore, caution should be exercised in interpreting that all educational programs are beneficial to children" (Madigan et al., 2020, n.p.). As discussed earlier in this chapter, the term "educational" refers to many types of children's apps and programs. No agreed-on standard exists to determine what apps promote learning, making it difficult for families to know whether educational claims have any real validity.

Reading Skills. A newer area for investigation is the impact of screen media on the process of learning to read, which usually occurs between the ages of 4 and 8. Emerging research corroborates what elementary school educators have noticed—that as screen exposure and use have increased, children seem more easily distracted and have a harder time comprehending what they read (Heubeck, 2024). Neurobiologists have found an association between increased screen use and lower white-matter integrity in the areas of the brain associated with language development and emergent literacy in preschoolers (Hutton et al., 2019). White-matter integrity is important for efficient signal connections between areas of the brain, and lower white-matter integrity is cause for concern. If parts of the brain associated with language and literacy don't connect as efficiently, the ability to learn to read is deterred. As neurobiologist Tzipi Horowitz-Kraus notes,

"Brain connectivity known to enhance reading and associated cognition appears to be weaker among children who are reading print less and engaging in screen time more" (quoted in Heubeck, 2024, n.p.). At the same time, literacy experts worry that the omnipresence of screens is overstimulating children and negatively impacting their ability to focus. A higher level of distractibility reduces their willingness or ability to concentrate on extracting meaning from what they are reading (Heubeck, 2024).

In addition to concerns about focus, research indicates that reading on screens rather than from printed books has a negative impact on comprehension. In 2023, an analysis of 26 recent K–12 and college reading studies found a correlation between reading on screens and lower comprehension skills in elementary and middle school students. The researchers describe the texts used in many digital reading activities as being of "low linguistic quality" and speculate that frequent exposure to such texts may prevent early readers from building a strong foundation. "For example," they note, "early readers engaging in frequent digital reading may learn less academic vocabulary and syntax, or develop to a lesser extent the ability to keep focused on a task, in a critical period when they are shifting from learning to read to reading to learn" (Altamura et al., 2023). Given the increased amount of time children spend reading on screens in school, the researchers recommend further study of this practice on students' comprehension and reading skills.

Problematic Media Use

Researchers use the term problematic media use (PMU) to describe excessive media use that interferes with normative functioning. PMU can develop for individuals of all ages, impacting their quality of life and relationships. Parental PMU is recognized as a significant variable in the development of child PMU, and the family environment has been identified as a key factor in raising the chances of child PMU (Swit et al., 2023). Child PMU is characterized by the excessive use of screen media devices that interferes with children's social, behavioral, or academic functioning (Rega et al., 2023). Researchers note that spending a large amount of time using media should not be mistaken for PMU. Manifestations of PMU in young children include

- preoccupation with media use;
- withdrawal from other activities;
- increased tolerance for prolonged media use;
- parental difficulty in placing and enforcing limits on children's media use;
- media use as a mechanism to cope with difficult emotions;
- child dishonesty about media use;
- loss of relationships due to media use; and
- psychosocial problems due to media use (Domoff et al., 2019).

Children who face psychological challenges, strained relationships with their parents, and difficulties in school are more likely to develop PMU. PMU is shown to lead to various harmful effects on children's development and well-being, such as increased behavioral issues, sleep disturbances, heightened depressive symptoms, reduced emotional intelligence, and lower academic performance (Rega et al., 2023).

THE BENEFITS OF RESEARCH-INFORMED PRACTICE

The research findings described in this chapter provide useful background for understanding the complexities of children's screen time, exposure, and use, as well as for counteracting the pervasive influence of screen myths. We have used research that meets the important standard of being peer-reviewed by colleagues in the same field and published in professional journals. It can be challenging, though, for early childhood practitioners to access current research across a range of disciplines, or to recognize which findings are most significant for children or relevant for their practice. Often research findings are oversimplified or distorted when reported in popular media, which can lead to confusion or misconceptions that can be difficult to dislodge. Here are a few considerations and suggestions for practitioners who want to use research findings effectively to inform their work with children and families:

- *Most of the research about the impact of screen media on young children is correlational, not causal.* The research may indicate associations between screen exposure and a desired (or undesired) effect, but associations or correlations can exist without being causal. For example, researchers have found a correlation between excessive television viewing in infancy and attention problems later in childhood. This does not prove, however, that early television viewing causes attention disorders.
- *Research findings are more robust when similar effects are found over time in multiple studies.* A good example of this is the still face experiment, described earlier in this chapter, which has been replicated many times since Edward Tronick first introduced it in the 1970s (Tronick et al., 1978). This replication creates a strong body of evidence that infants react negatively (and quickly) when parents withdraw attention.
- *Some research studies, especially in education, often involve small sample sizes of a few children or take the form of case studies.* Findings from these studies may provide insights, but they may not be easily replicated or applicable across wider populations.
- *Many research studies are conducted in lab settings under carefully designed and monitored conditions.* While the findings may provide

useful insights, they may not be relevant to natural settings like classrooms or to the needs and capacities of individual children. Studies conducted in classroom settings under naturalistic conditions are especially useful for educators.

- *Popular press reports about research findings may include links or references to the original study.* Reviewing the original study, especially the Discussion and Conclusion sections, can provide more accurate information.
- *Tech products marketed for children often include broad or vague claims that they are backed by "research."* These claims can be taken with a grain of salt, as the research is often done in-house and funded by the product manufacturer. Such research does not entail the same rigorous review process as peer-reviewed research findings published in professional journals.

Practitioners who want to keep current with the research will find it helpful to become familiar with the names of well-known and respected researchers. Many of those researchers are cited in this chapter and elsewhere in this book. Their work also informs guidelines established by professional associations such as the American Academy of Pediatrics and the World Health Organization. Other organizations are known for specific areas of research on screen media; for example, Common Sense Media regularly conducts national surveys to gain information about the current state of children's media use, and the Pew Research Center publishes social science research on media, parenting, and screen use. Knowing about these individuals and organizations can guide practitioners toward reliable sources of information and insight.

The early childhood field is well equipped with knowledge on nurturing young children's development. Practitioners can draw on that knowledge and their own expertise when reviewing research findings and weighing the implications for children. Engaging with research enables practitioners to make informed decisions about screen use in their settings and provide helpful guidance and resources for colleagues and families.

QUESTIONS FOR REFLECTION

1. What screen myth(s) have you encountered in your own life or in your work with children and families?
2. What actions could you take to address or debunk the myth(s) you have identified?

3. Of the research findings discussed in this chapter, what was most interesting to you? Most surprising? What do you want to know more about?
4. What is one way you can envision utilizing research on the impacts of screen time, exposure, and/or use in your work with young children or their families?

CHAPTER 4

Promoting Protective Factors

The SAFEC principle Protection-Oriented ensures that children's well-being and safety—physical, emotional, relational, and environmental—guide decisions about screen time and use. In this chapter, we discuss safeguards for children and families, describe the role and power of protective factors, and explore how family protective factors can reduce technology-related stressors and vulnerabilities. We also introduce our five Screen-Aware Protective Factors, research-based priorities for fostering healthy outcomes, promoting resilience, and mitigating harm.

A STRENGTHS-BASED LENS

Debates about the impacts of screen-based devices and media often take place on a continuum between what media literacy educator and advocate Faith Rogow (2023) describes as the "moral panic" following the release of new media technologies on one end, and the wholesale embrace of them as "salvation" on the other (p. 8). There is little argument, though, that concrete harms and *risk factors*—conditions that pose challenges or threats to individuals, families, or communities—exist. The discussion of child developmental needs in Chapter 2 and examination of research in Chapter 3 reveal areas of serious concern, but focusing exclusively on the risks and negative impacts of screens can be exhausting, discouraging, and even counterproductive.

Strengths-based approaches provide a proven alternative to problem-based approaches. In the strengths-based paradigm, risk factors are acknowledged as existing and difficult but, importantly, are not viewed as determinants. Instead, they are considered within the broader context of strengths and resources that can be mobilized to foster resilience, well-being, and positive outcomes. Understanding risk factors and negative outcomes is important, but not an end goal. Rather, the knowledge of risks and harms is a step toward building on existing strengths, developing new strengths, and strengthening the conditions within the larger social environment. Unlike approaches focused on identifying and correcting problems and deficiencies, strengths-based approaches acknowledge that individuals, families, and communities possess and can cultivate *protective factors*—unique attributes, abilities, and capacities—that can be leveraged to address risk factors and promote positive outcomes (Maton et al., 2004).

FAMILY PROTECTIVE FACTORS AND SCREEN AWARENESS

Protections are created when stakeholders identify and promote variables that address and reduce risks and work together to design, implement, and evaluate needed interventions (Maton et al., 2004). Psychiatrist Carl Bell, known for his work on community mental health and violence prevention, introduced a frequently referenced maxim that "risk factors are not predictive factors because of protective factors" (Almeida, 2019). Promoting evidence-based protective factors is shown to mitigate stress, foster resilience, support healthy development, and promote positive child, adult, and family functioning, especially in times of adversity (Leadbeater et al., 2004).

A specific strengths-based approach that translates well into screen awareness is the Strengthening Families approach, designed by the Center for the Study of Social Policy (CSSP). The approach recognizes the strengths that each family already possesses and builds on them to bolster child and family well-being in both the short and long term. Strengthening Families promotes the research-based family protective factors of parental resilience, social connections, knowledge of parenting and child development, social and emotional competence of children, and concrete support in times of need. The Strengthening Families approach, and its emphasis on family protective factors, provides relief from stressors like economic hardship, illness, and trauma. It is used in child care environments, schools, health systems, faith communities, neighborhoods, and public policy.

Like the Strengthening Families approach, the Screen-Aware Framework for Early Childhood prioritizes relationships and protective factors, honoring parents' knowledge of their own children and their own circumstances and helping parents feel respected, not judged. The family plays an early and critical role in shaping children's experiences with digital media. As detailed in the following sections, screens can contribute to family stress but can also serve as tools to help families build protective skills. When families can identify and find relief from stressors, they gain increased capacity to build on their strengths to mitigate digital harms.

Parental Resilience

Aisha, a social worker, has fallen behind on her work due to a difficult case. The stress has led to a few sleepless nights, and she feels exhausted. Her boss asks her to stay late and complete a client report. By the time she arrives 30 minutes late to pick up her son, Devin, at child care, he is the only child left and is sobbing. In the car, Aisha is tempted to hand Devin a tablet set to a preschool game to soothe him. She knows that devices are not the best way to calm a child, but she struggles to think of another way.

Instead of handing Devin a device, Aisha remembers what she learned at her parenting classes: After a long day, children crave time with their parent(s). Despite a throbbing headache, she asks him questions about his day and takes deep breaths when he throws crackers. Aisha calls her neighbor. "Would you mind coming over to play with Devin for 20 minutes while I take a short nap? I haven't been sleeping and I know I'll have a better evening with him if I can just put my head down." Her neighbor agrees.

After her nap, Aisha cooks dinner and manages Devin's bedtime routine without using the tablet or television. She realizes she needed time with Devin as much as he needed time with her. She accesses her resilience by using her knowledge and asking for help.

The American Psychological Association defines resilience as the process and outcome of successfully adapting to difficult or challenging life experiences, especially through mental, emotional, and behavioral flexibility and adjustment to external and internal demands. A common assumption is that resilience is a character trait that people either have or they don't. On the contrary, resilience is a skill built while managing and bouncing back from adversity. Resilience provides two-generation and even multigeneration benefits. When practitioners assist families in building resilience, adults and children are better equipped to experience the deep personal connection they need to thrive.

When families face stressful circumstances and events, like economic hardship, burdensome child care expenses, elder care responsibilities, illness, or trauma, their capacity to manage their children's screen use can be compromised. Parents may rely on screens more, either for themselves or their children. This apparent solution to stress can backfire, creating more problems than it solves. In stressful times, children need direct involvement from parents and other loving adults, acknowledgment that current circumstances might be difficult, and assurance that they are loved and cared for. Parental resilience can lower reliance on devices in trying circumstances and, in doing so, strengthen bonds between parents and children.

Higher levels of parental screen use are correlated with higher levels of child screen use (Cost et al., 2023). Research has also connected high-volume screen use and depressive symptoms in mothers. Having a depressed mother in the household was associated with double the amount of television viewing. Depressed mothers reported being less likely to sit and talk with their children during television use or to consult outside sources for information and advice on managing screen media. This increase in infant and young child screen time and exposure without corresponding parental involvement could negatively affect the children's developmental outcomes (Bank et al., 2012).

Understanding parental behaviors around screen use can help practitioners to support parental resilience by focusing on building strengths. One potential benefit of the Internet is that it can provide unprecedented access to support when stressful events impact a family. Online resources for grief, domestic abuse, and mental health allow parents to access help when children are in school or in bed, rather than during children's waking hours. When extended families live at a distance, virtual connections and communications with caring family members can provide comfort and support. Parents can increase resilience by seeking online education and training that could lead to greater career opportunities, providing feelings of accomplishment and a path to greater income.

Social Connections

Antony oversees an after-school program that serves about 60 students in kindergarten through grade 3. When parents sign their children up for the program, they complete a short survey about their child's interests. Antony uses this information to plan activities, clubs, and events for the children. The survey also asks families to indicate any questions or concerns.

In reviewing the survey information for the upcoming school year, Antony notices that several parents asked about whether their children will be using screens during the after-school program and expressed concerns about adding to their children's screen time. Antony feels confident that he can assure parents that the after-school program emphasizes play, outdoor and physical activity, and creativity. He also wants to support families in managing their children's screen time.

During the first weeks of the school year, Antony distributes handouts with information, resources, and suggestions about screen-free activities for children ages 5–8 and their families. Antony also offers a short workshop for parents about strategies for managing screen time. At the workshop, several parents who want to adopt the strategies exchange contact information. They agree to support each other as they try to limit their children's screen time. Throughout the coming months, the families use a group chat to share ideas, coach one another through challenges, and celebrate successes. The approach is so effective that Antony invites them to lead a workshop at the end of the school year about managing children's screen time during the summer months.

Parents' access to healthy social support increases resilience and benefits both adults and children. Companionship, community, and practical support, which may include help accessing financial assistance, transportation, and education, exemplify this protective factor. The Strengthening Families approach emphasizes that all parents need nonjudgmental family, friends, neighbors, co-workers, and community members who care about them and their children (Browne, 2014). These social connections provide a buffering effect for parents' and children's well-being when families face stressful situations (Hostinar & Gunnar, 2015). For parents of young children, a sense of belonging and connection within classroom and school communities can prevent isolation and foster healthy attachments and reciprocal positive regard (Browne, 2014).

When school and neighborhood groups discuss screen challenges together, parents can share tips, strategies, and encouragement. Implementing screen management can cause an initial upset for children and require a period of transition and patience while families try new routines. Children may have tantrums or express frustration and need a few days or weeks to incorporate new expectations into their routine. When establishing screen time rules increases discord and stress, parents may be tempted to give up. But when parents engage with others, they can find comfort in sharing successes and failures. Also, children who have similar parameters as their peers don't feel ostracized, but part of a system that provides consistency and affirmation for screen choices.

Digital platforms can provide helpful online support in a world where many live away from family. Online communities can affirm parenting choices, especially supporting new parents and parents of children with disabilities. Video chat with family and friends can provide essential touchpoints of encouragement for parents under stress. Social connections are not only about getting help, but also feeling a sense of purpose in giving help. Ideally, social networks are reciprocal. Screen-aware online communities support one another in learning about technology and sharing their frustrations and successes in minimizing the impact on their children.

Knowledge of Parenting and Child Development

Three-year-old Tasha wakes every morning expecting to hear the whirr of a blender and get a taste of homemade juice. This Monday morning her parents, Rosa and Adam, are struggling to start the day. Rosa, 9 months pregnant, has slept very little, and they were both awake much of the night. When Tasha bounds into the bedroom at 6:15 a.m. saying, "juice time?," Rosa and Adam groan. "Go put the TV on, Tash," Adam says.

Giving it a second thought, Adam gets out of bed. He remembers that routines are important to 3-year-olds. He is also unsure whether Tasha will choose an appropriate show to watch. As soon as she hears her dad start the juice blender, Tasha makes her way to the kitchen, full of stories about her friends at school and questions about where the new baby will sleep. Adam feels tired but good, knowing he is providing some predictability for Tasha, especially during this time of transition.

Children benefit when parents and practitioners understand key developmental needs and recognize their role in supporting the best possible outcomes. While there is no such thing as a perfect parent, the Strengthening Families approach explains that certain parenting behaviors are considered essential for healthy child development. This approach also acknowledges that every parent knows their child best, empowering them to adapt and adjust their parenting style to their child's temperament and specific needs.

Research has found that children thrive when parents or caregivers provide the following fundamental experiences:

- Safety: keep children secure from physical or psychological harm.
- Stability: provide predictability and consistency in a child's social, emotional, and physical environment.
- Nurturing: consistently meet children's needs.
- Time and Commitment: spend quality time with children and advocate on their behalf.
- Resources: provide financial, psychological, emotional, and social resources.
- Skills and knowledge: acquire education, training, interactions with child-related professionals, and personal experiences.

(Centers for Disease Control, 2024)

Knowledge of child development applies to screen use in ways researchers are just beginning to understand. Emerging brain imaging technology, employed by researcher John Hutton at Cincinnati Children's Hospital, indicates that early digital media use impacts brain development in areas responsible for visual processing, empathy, attention, complex memory, and early reading skills (Hutton et al., 2019). Providing safety, then, also means keeping children safe from early and frequent screen use that may harm their brain development. When parents become familiar with children's developmental needs and processes, they can apply that knowledge to screen use. For example, if caregivers understand that a 3-year-old needs 10–13 hours of sleep, then they will avoid incorporating tablet use during bedtime routines because screens excite the brain and keep the child awake longer. While applying child developmental priorities to parenting behaviors, it's important to consider context, which may include stressors and challenges that make "doing our best" the primary goal in screen management and in other parenting tasks.

The Internet, social media, podcasts, and parenting apps can support parents in learning about parenting and child development without having to read volumes. Short videos by organizations like the Brazelton Institute, Zero to Three, and the Centers for Disease Control provide digestible, practical information, as does the social media commentary of educational consultant Dan Wuori (Goldstein, 2024). Online communities of parents share tips and experiences that translate easily into daily application. The Screen Aware Early Childhood Action Kit, highlighted in Part II of this book, is an example of a free, online, open-source resource that provides parent-centered information.

Social-Emotional Competence of Children

Eighteen-month-old Zev finds transitions challenging, and his mother, Marsha, has a hard time getting him dressed and out the door each morning. After being reprimanded several times for being late to work, Marsha resorts to letting Zev watch videos on her phone while she changes and dresses him and gets him in the car for child care drop-off. Zev insists on watching the phone throughout the car ride and screams when Marsha takes her phone back at the door of the child care program. Marsha hates that she and Zev are starting the day off battling with each other and worries about exposing him to additional screen time. Zev has recently qualified for early intervention services. During her first meeting with Leah, the early intervention specialist, Marsha shares her concerns about the morning ordeal. She gratefully accepts Leah's offer to come by one morning to observe and then work with the family to make mornings less stressful.

During the observation, Leah notices that giving Zev the phone is preventing him from being engaged in a morning routine; instead, he is passively staring at the screen while his mother changes, dresses, and carries him to the car. Leah suggests another approach. She takes photos of articles of Zev's clothing and his outerwear and compiles them into a short book called Zev Gets Ready, *with a photo of Zev on the cover. Each page of the book features one item of clothing—diaper, shirt, pants, socks, shoes, coat, hat—and a few words. The last page says, "Zev is ready to go!" under a picture of the car.*

The next morning, Leah encourages Marsha to read the book with Zev and then use the book to guide him through each step of getting ready. Several times Zev asks, "Phone?" but Marsha and Leah redirect him to the book and ask, "What's next for Zev?" Zev wants to take the book in the car with him to child care and shows it to his teacher when he arrives. Marsha continues to use the book in the mornings until Zev has become familiar with the routine and doesn't need the cues anymore (though he still loves to look at the photos). Marsha reports to Leah that Zev has responded so well to following these visual cues that she has created a similar photo book for their nighttime routine. Having the books reminds Marsha of the importance of involving her son in daily routines.

Social-emotional competence is an essential task of childhood because it impacts all other areas of development (American Academy of Pediatrics, 2022). Supporting children's social and emotional competence enhances protection not only in childhood but throughout their adult lives. This protective factor develops when children grow up in environments and with experiences that enable them to form close, secure adult and peer relationships and to regulate and constructively express their emotions. Beginning in infancy, children develop social-emotional competence that builds self-esteem, self-efficacy, self-regulation, executive functioning, intrinsic motivation, conflict resolution, social, and communication skills. With healthy social-emotional competence, children learn to understand and identify their own feelings, accurately read and comprehend the emotions of others, regulate their own behavior, develop empathy for others, and establish and sustain healthy relationships.

When parents and practitioners foster social and emotional intelligence, children are more likely to function and adapt well in school, form successful friendships and intimate relationships, and eventually succeed at parenting, hold a job, and become a contributing member of society (Browne, 2014). Parents and educators can help children develop social-emotional competence by reading and identifying children's emotional cues, modeling appropriate behavior, showing consideration for their desires and needs, respecting their viewpoints, expressing interest and pride in their activities, and providing encouragement in times of stress. Providing interactive, language-rich environments and opportunities to explore and learn by doing also supports the development of social-emotional competence (Browne, 2014). As with each of the protective factors, the relational aspect of social-emotional competence supports resilience and mitigates the harms of early screen use.

Concrete Support in Times of Need

Beth is a single parent of two active children, ages 3 and 5. She works full-time in an elder care facility. After she and her partner split up, Beth and the children moved in with her aunt, Maria. Beth feels fortunate to live with Maria, whom she thinks of as a parent. Both children attend Head Start every weekday morning, and Maria cares for them in the afternoons. Lately, Beth has been coming home from work to find both children cuddled on the couch with Maria with the television on. Often, Maria seems to be waking from a nap. Beth worries that caring for the children may be too much for Maria. She isn't happy that they are spending so much time in front of the TV and is concerned about imposing on her aunt, but feels she doesn't have many options.

Beth realizes she must take action to improve the situation for Maria and the children. She begins by talking with Maria, who says she adores the children but finds their energy a bit overwhelming. She admits that caring for them every day makes her so tired that she has been keeping the TV on all afternoon to keep them quiet. Beth then reaches out to other family members to see if anyone can help. One of her cousins who attends a nearby community college offers to pick up the children once a week and take care of them to give Maria a day off; another, younger cousin says he will come by once a week to help Maria with the children. Beth also talks with her boss, who agrees to change her schedule so that she works Tuesdays through Saturdays, freeing her up to be with the children on Mondays, and Beth's ex says he will care for the children at his mother's house every Saturday. Beth then talks with the Head Start program staff, who provide resources about screen-free activities with preschoolers and managing screen time, which Beth shares with Maria. Beth now needs Maria to watch the children three afternoons a week, rather than five, and Maria will have help on one of those afternoons. This arrangement is comfortable, if complicated, and Beth feels that she has avoided overburdening Maria while reducing her children's screen time. Although she knows that she'll have to adjust the arrangements during the weeks when Head Start is not in session, and again when her older child starts kindergarten, Beth feels more confident that she can rely on family members and others for support.

All parents need help, whether facing the routine challenges of raising a family or dealing with stressful situations like unemployment, illness, substance abuse, or food insecurity. The Strengthening Families approach focuses on three pillars that enable families to get concrete support:

1. self-advocacy and asking for help;
2. availability and accessibility of resources; and
3. high-quality service delivery.

Most of the family protective factors have overlapping benefits. For instance, asking for help can build resilience. When seeking help, parents and caregivers look for both formal and informal support systems. However, many communities have unequal access to the formal supports of education, housing, and employment. Research shows that families do better when they live near relatives and/or close friends or in strong, supportive communities—the informal supports. Building neighborhood and community capacity is a protective strategy that many agencies use to create informal supports while providing the formal supports of education, housing, jobs, and training.

The need for both formal and informal support applies to screen use as well. When it comes to early screen management, many families and practitioners don't know how or where to ask for help. The resources in the second part of this book highlight organizations that offer concrete support—like free, accessible information, webinars, and tip sheets—for managing screens. Position statements and guidelines by the American Academy of Pediatrics, Zero to Three, the World Health Organization, and the American Speech-Language-Hearing Association provide solid guidance. Informal supports such as parent groups and neighborhood- and school-based organizations satisfy the need for peer support. Parenting blogs, apps, podcasts, and social media sites can help prevent feelings of isolation. For example, online content produced by parent educators provides relevant and useful information such as examples of programming that overstimulates children contrasted with more developmentally appropriate, slower-paced, and calming options. These sites also offer little "life hacks" that help parents reduce screen use by encouraging more play with common everyday household items. Knowing that other parents and practitioners struggle with screen management can make families feel less alone. While there is useful information online, not all content creators are experts drawing from research. Practitioners can provide helpful, evidence-based recommendations for families.

SCREEN-AWARE PROTECTIVE FACTORS

Strengths-based frameworks recognize that children, families, and communities continuously encounter challenges and harness existing strengths as they develop new skills and understandings (Leadbeater et al., 2004). They also emphasize that activating protective variables ensures that children have the conditions and safety to thrive. SAFEC, as a strengths-based framework, builds on the understanding that when adults feel active, supported, and knowledgeable about screen use, children are less susceptible to the harms. Our research-based Screen-Aware Protective Factors highlight five top priorities for reducing risks, increasing positive adaptations, and promoting child and adult well-being in a screen-dominated world.

Five Screen-Aware Protective Factors

1. Responsive Relationships
2. Offline Play and Physical Activity
3. Time Outdoors and in Nature
4. Critical Media Literacy Practices
5. Resources for Empowerment

Screen-Aware Protective Factor 1: Responsive Relationships

Being in responsive relationships with caring adults is one of the most effective ways to protect children from harmful screen use. Responsive relationships provide children with emotional security and strengthen their resilience and capacity to handle challenges. Responsive, nonromantic relationships between adults, described as those in which the participants are "warm, sensitive to their partners' feelings, and want to make their partners feel comfortable, valued, listened to, and understood," are also advantageous (Canvello & Crocker, 2010, p. 2). Such relationships emphasize understanding, caring, and support. When these qualities exist in relationships between parents and early childhood practitioners, practitioners and their colleagues, or practitioners and administrators, the relationship can provide validation and encouragement for promoting children's well-being.

It is all too easy to get immersed in or distracted by screens. Being aware of, and working to minimize, the potential dangers of technoference and working to boost opportunities for joint media engagement are powerful ways to enhance responsive relationships in the digital age (see Chapter 5). The following sections describe some of the ways in which responsive relationships can serve as a protective factor for child and adult screen use.

Promoting Learning. Many families introduce young children to apps and programs believing that these will promote children's learning. They may not be aware, however, that research clearly shows that older toddlers and preschoolers are much more likely to learn from screens when the content is scaffolded by responsive, caring adults. For infants and toddlers, there is little evidence that apps or games that claim to be educational have *any* benefit, especially when young children are using the apps on their own. Children ages 2½ to 3 and younger experience what researchers call a "transfer deficit," meaning that they find it challenging or impossible to transfer what they see or learn in 2D (screen) encounters to the 3D (real) world, and vice versa (Barr et al., 2019). But toddlers ages 18 months and older are more likely to be able to transfer their learning in situations where an adult engages with them in a process called *joint media engagement.* They need the support of a responsive, engaged adult to facilitate their ability to transfer information between 2D and 3D contexts by scaffolding the experience using joint media engagement strategies (Zack & Barr, 2016).

Simple co-viewing, such as watching a TV program or looking at an app together, is not as effective in promoting children's learning as joint media engagement strategies—talking about what is on the screen, labeling and describing objects and actions, asking questions, and making connections to the child's own experiences. These strategies also help older children make meaning from screen content. Learning and utilizing effective joint media engagement skills can empower family members who want young children to derive the most benefit from their encounters with screens (see Chapter 5).

Three-year-old Lalie is allowed to watch half an hour of television a day, as long as one of the adult members of the family is available to watch with her. That person is often her father, Moses. As they watch Lalie's favorite program, her father asks questions such as, "What do you think is going to happen now?" and "How do you think that character is feeling?" Moses observes Lalie closely to see how she's reacting to the program. One day, a character on the show looks out the window and says, "It's raining cats and dogs!" Moses can tell from Lalie's expression that she is puzzled by the phrase. He tells her that when people say, "it's raining cats and dogs," they don't mean that cats and dogs are actually falling down from the sky, but that it's raining very hard. "Remember the day we got caught on the playground and we had to run to the car and by the time we got there we were soaking wet and left puddles on the car seats? And our shoes were so wet we had to dry them on the radiator? That's the kind of rain people mean when they say it's raining cats and dogs." The next time it rains hard, Moses asks Lalie, "What do you think about this rain?" "Cats and dogs! Cats and dogs!" she replies with delight.

Providing Understanding and Support. Families cannot control or even be aware of every screen encounter that their children experience, especially as children get older. Some screen encounters may confuse, disturb, or upset the child. Responsive adults are more likely to notice when a child is having these feelings—as expressed in their drawings or writings, their play, or their talk. Responsive relationships ensure that children can open up about distressing screen content and adults can take action to prevent recurrences of such encounters.

Early childhood professionals can more effectively partner with parents if they avoid judgment or the appearance of judgment and assume they both want the children's well-being. In relationships based on good faith and shared goals, partners are more willing to discuss their fears and concerns and provide support to allay each other's fears and concerns. Families will more readily reach out to practitioners with questions and concerns related to screen use and will be more open to information and suggestions. Practitioners will also be more willing to talk with colleagues and administrators when they feel overwhelmed or confused in navigating the screenscape, or to bring up their own questions and concerns.

Priya notices that one of her first-grade students, Felix, has been exhibiting some unusual behaviors lately. He has been drawing "bad guys" wearing masks and telling other children how he's going to fight the bad guys. Felix has been a calm and friendly child, but now he sometimes startles other children by putting his hands up in front of his face and growling. One day she finds him demonstrating his "moves" to a small cluster of other children and must intervene before he accidentally kicks another child. At recess time she asks Felix to sit with her and says, "I noticed you have been talking about fighting, Felix. Is something worrying you?" Felix mumbles something about bad guys and says earnestly, "We have to fight them so they can't get us." Priya assures him that there are no bad guys in their class and that her job is to keep him and the other children safe. She says, "I know you would never want to accidentally hurt one of your friends, because you care about them." Felix promises not to do his moves near other children.

Priya calls Felix's mother and describes his behavior and their conversation to her. She tells Felix's mom that this new behavior doesn't seem like him at all. Felix's mother expresses surprise at first, but then says, "You know, now that you mention it, Felix has seemed a bit jumpy and anxious lately, especially at bedtime. My younger brother has been staying with us and I thought maybe Felix was just excited to have him here. He really loves my brother." She tells Priya she'll talk more with Felix to try to find out what's bothering him.

The next day, Priya gets an email from Felix's mom: "Thanks so much for letting me know about Felix's concerns about bad guys. Turns out my brother has been showing Felix wrestling videos on his phone. I didn't realize that they were doing that. My brother loves being with Felix but he doesn't know much about what's appropriate for kids. He says he just wanted to share something he loves with Felix.

I've talked with him and Felix about why it's not a good idea for them to watch these videos, and we've come up with a list of other things they can do together. I'm also reassuring Felix that my brother and I will keep him safe. I really appreciate that Felix felt comfortable to share his feelings with you and that you contacted me."

Screen-Aware Protective Factor 2: Offline Play and Physical Activity

Play and physical activity greatly benefit the well-being of children and adults and serve as powerful protective factors against potentially harmful effects of screen use. Play and physical activity are also closely linked. Health care professionals and child development experts have noted with alarm the significant decline over the last few decades in the time children spend playing and being active, which corresponds with steady increases in their time using screens (North, 2023; Yogman et al., 2018).

Time for play and physical activity has also severely declined in schools, especially during the last 2 decades. The No Child Left Behind Act of 2001 mandated early literacy and math focus in preschool and the primary grades, resulting in reduced recess and play (Rix, 2022). Dramatic play and block play areas, previously staples of preschool and kindergarten classrooms, disappeared in many schools as unstructured recess and indoor free play began to be considered distractions from instructional time. Yet research shows that school-age children pay attention better after free physical play at recess. Free play supports attention more than structured physical education activities, probably because children are more active during free play (Yogman et al., 2018). Additional health benefits from physically active free play include enhancing children's immune, endocrine, and cardiovascular systems; reducing depression; decreasing stress and fatigue; and increasing range of motion, agility, coordination, balance, and flexibility (Yogman et al., 2018).

Screen use during the pandemic impacted children's play and physical activity, too. In 2021, researchers published a review of 17 studies about the impact of COVID-19 on children in North America and Europe. Overall, the research indicated that screen time use among children increased for leisure activities as well as education purposes. The more devices that were available at home, the more likely it was that children spent their leisure time on screens. But the more that parents discouraged screen use, the more their children engaged in play (Kourti et al., 2021).

Limiting Sedentary Screen Time. Ensuring that young children have more time and opportunities for physical activity is a valuable way to promote their health and well-being. Being sedentary puts children at greater risk for serious health problems in later life, such as heart disease, diabetes, and some forms of cancer, as well as mental health issues (Tremblay et al., 2015). It also increases children's exposure to advertising and consumerism.

The World Health Organization (WHO) guidelines make a clear association between increased time on screens and negative impacts on children's health, especially regarding sleep. Children of all ages, beginning in infancy, are sleeping less than in previous generations. Higher levels of physical activity, however, are associated with better-quality sleep and more sleep. The WHO guidelines (2019 and 2020) recommend limits on screen time as well as daily minimum times for physical activity, by age group, as follows:

- Infants under 1 year should be physically active several times a day in a variety of ways, particularly through interactive floor-based play; more is better. For those not yet mobile, this includes at least 30 minutes in prone position (tummy time) spread throughout the day while awake. Screen time is not recommended.
- Children 1–2 years of age should spend at least 180 minutes in a variety of physical activities at any intensity, including moderate- to vigorous-intensity physical activity, spread throughout the day; more is better. For 1-year-olds, sedentary screen time (such as watching TV or videos, playing computer games) is not recommended. For those aged 2 years, sedentary screen time should be no more than 1 hour; less is better.
- Children 3–4 years of age should spend at least 180 minutes in a variety of physical activities at any intensity, of which at least 60 minutes is moderate- to vigorous-intensity physical activity, spread throughout the day; more is better. Sedentary screen time should be no more than 1 hour; less is better.
- Children 5–17 years of age should accumulate at least 60 minutes of moderate- to vigorous-intensity physical activity each day; most of this physical activity should be aerobic. Children should limit the amount of time spent being sedentary, particularly recreational screen time.

Promoting Play. Intrinsically motivated, engaging, freely chosen, pleasurable, and imaginative play is also a powerful protective factor against the developmental vulnerabilities associated with screen use. Concerns about declining play in children's daily lives and recognition of its many developmental benefits prompted the American Academy of Pediatrics (AAP) to issue a clinical report, *The Power of Play,* in 2018. "Play is not frivolous," the report clearly states, "it is brain building" (Yogman et al., 2018, p. 5).

The AAP report cites extensive research establishing the many developmental benefits associated with play. As the report notes, "Media (e.g., television, video games, and smartphone and tablet applications) use often encourages passivity and the consumption of others' creativity rather than active learning and socially active play" (Yogman et al., 2018, p. 8). Play has the power to

- promote brain development and learning;
- build language and early math skills;
- encourage positive relationships between children and adult caregivers and children and their peers;
- strengthen the development of self-regulation, impulse control, and emotional regulation;
- help children develop a sense of independence and agency;
- enhance emotional and social competencies as children negotiate roles and directions for their play;
- reduce stress (and help prevent toxic stress that can threaten brain development);
- provide safe opportunities for children to process stressful or confusing experiences;
- promote physical activity that benefits overall health;
- enhance curiosity, creativity, attention, memory, and problem-solving—all associated with learning; and
- reflect and teach cultural values.

Play and physical activity can support adults, too. In addition to the physical benefits of increased activity, exercise helps strengthen adult brains and enhance mental health (Smith, 2024). Play has similar health benefits for adults as it does for children. It reduces stress, brightens mood, increases energy, enhances creativity, helps maintain social well-being, and keeps the mind sharp (Robinson et al., 2024). And when adult caregivers play with children, they build responsive relationships and support their own and the child's well-being.

Screen-Aware Protective Factor 3: Time Outdoors and in Nature

A major change to childhood in the United States over the last several decades has been the dramatic decline in the amount of time that children spend outdoors and in nature. Several factors influenced this decline. In the early 1980s, a few high-profile cases of child abduction or harm, corresponding with the advent of round-the-clock cable news, caused parents to worry about children's safety. Exaggerated safety concerns, as well as fears of possible litigation from playground accidents, led to fewer public outdoor play spaces. As more women joined the workforce, the number of so-called "latchkey" children increased; many parents believed these children would be safer indoors than playing outside without adult supervision. In schools, academic pressures stemming from the requirements of the No Child Left Behind legislation enacted in 2001 and Race to the Top regulations instituted in 2009 led to more math and literacy instruction and less outdoor recess.

Active outdoor play and time in nature act as key protective factors to mitigate the impact of sedentary screen time on children and adults. Some of the benefits of outdoor time are described in the following sections.

Increased Physical Activity. Multiple research studies have found a positive association between time spent outdoors and increased physical activity (Dankiw et al., 2020; Larouche et al., 2016). It is important to note that *free* play outdoors provides more health benefits than structured outdoor play. The Position Statement on Active Outdoor Play published in 2015 by a group of eminent Canadian researchers clearly states: "When children are closely supervised outside, they are less active" (Tremblay et al., 2015).

Enhanced Emotional and Social Resilience. A systematic review of many studies on outdoor play in nature noted the positive effects on children's emotional and social resilience (Dankiw et al., 2020). Access to nature and time spent in nature serves as a buffer to reduce the impact of stress (Wells & Evans, 2003). Studies have also found that time spent outdoors in nature reduces anger and aggression and improves children's social interactions (Bravender & Bravender, 2020). One study compared two Los Angeles school playgrounds, one of which contained traditional playground features while the other provided more natural elements. Students at the school with the natural playground demonstrated a significant decrease in physical and verbal conflicts compared to their peers using the traditional playground (Raney et al., 2023). The researchers speculate that one possible reason for fewer conflicts in the natural play area was that the children there engaged in more imaginative and unstructured play rather than playing prescriptive games with rules.

Enhanced Curiosity, Imagination, and Creativity. Research on time outdoors and in nature found that nature play positively impacted children's appreciation for the natural world, imagination, creativity, and dramatic play (Dankiw et al., 2020). Natural spaces inspire more curiosity than prefabricated playground structures, and sensory-rich natural environments help children practice problem-solving skills, creative thinking, and self-regulation (Tremblay et al., 2015).

Pediatric and public health associations recognize the importance of active outdoor play and provide advice and guidance for families and health professionals about increasing children's time outside. The research-based Canadian Position Statement on Active Outdoor Play for children ages 3–12 (Outdoor Play Canada, 2015) reminds families that "Outdoor play is safer than you think!" and that fears of harm from outdoor play tend to be exaggerated. Children potentially face more harm from staying indoors and engaging in sedentary screen use. In addition to the negative health effects of increased sedentary time, children could be exposed to inappropriate screen content, cyberpredators or cyberexploitation, and unhealthy eating (Outdoor Play Canada, 2015). Researchers have noted that spending more time outdoors engaged in active play increases children's sense of independence and self-esteem, as well as their ability to detect and manage risk (Tremblay et al., 2015).

Screen-Aware Protective Factor 4: Critical Media Literacy Practices

Adults play a crucial role in guiding children's understanding of the world around them, including making sense of the diverse forms of media they encounter. Adults, too, are immersed in increasingly complex media environments, including virtual ecosystems filled with AI-generated content and algorithm-driven social platforms, news, and entertainment. By expanding their own critical thinking and literacy skills, caregivers can be better prepared to help children become discerning, informed, and resilient media participants.

Critical media literacy combines media literacy abilities—synthesizing, analyzing, and producing mediated messages (National Association for Media Literacy Education, n.d.)—with awareness of the broader social, cultural, and political contexts in which media is produced. It emphasizes the interplay of information, knowledge, and power in the media and the influence of media on issues of identity and representation, including gender, race, class, sexuality, religion, age, and ability (Critical Media Project, n.d.). In doing so, critical media literacy serves as theory (as described in Chapter 1) and as "a transformative pedagogy for developing and empowering critical, caring, nurturing, and conscientious people" (Critical Media Project, n.d.).

Critical media literacy practices support what media education theorist Len Masterman (1985) describes as critical autonomy—the ability of individuals to critically analyze and evaluate media messages independently, without undue influence from external forces. Critical media literacy practices are protective because they empower adults and children to navigate media environments effectively, to identify and confront problematic media practices, and to make informed media choices centered on self-determination and individual, family, and community well-being (Share, 2015).

Benefits for Young Children and Families. Early childhood is a foundational period for developing skills, including those that will help children interpret media effectively and critically as they grow. With support, even young children can begin to understand basic media literacy concepts: Media are created (by people), using specific tools and techniques (e.g., colors, words, sounds, music) for specific reasons (e.g., entertainment, education, advertising, etc.), in ways intended to influence their feelings and interests (e.g., excitement, fear, curiosity, etc.).

Emphasizing similar convictions, the Technology in Early Childhood Center at the Erikson Institute hosted two national forums in 2019, bringing together organizations, experts, and practitioners with the aim of advancing media literacy in early childhood, family, and community education. Their resulting *Media Literacy in Early Childhood Report* highlights the importance of starting media literacy education early and introduces a framework, definition, and fundamental actions for early childhood media literacy (Herdzina & Lauricella, 2020). The report describes media literacy in early childhood as the emerging ability to

- Access: effectively locate, use, and select media.
- Engage and Explore: intentionally use media for purpose and enjoyment.
- Comprehend: understand media messages and practices and transfer that knowledge appropriately.
- Critically Inquire: question and analyze media messages.
- Evaluate: ask, "Is this media right for me or my task?"
- Create: make media with intention.

(Herdzina & Lauricella, 2020)

With adult guidance and modeling and through developmentally appropriate experiences, young children can be introduced to the fundamental actions of critical media literacy.

Three-year-old Liam has decided to be a lion for Halloween. After showing off his costume, his aunt suggests they watch a video of real lions together on the TV. Liam is thrilled, giggling and bouncing as playful music accompanies frolicking lion cubs. When the music slows and the sleepy cubs snuggle up to the mama lion, he climbs onto his aunt's lap for a cuddle. When the video shifts to footage of a male lion accompanied by suspenseful music, Liam covers his head and says he's done.

Noticing his reaction, his aunt pauses the video and says, "It seems like the music made that part a bit scarier, didn't it? Did you notice how the sounds changed with the big lion?" Liam nods. She explains that videos often use music to make us feel excited or nervous, and that he can take a break anytime. She then asks, "Would you like to go back to the part with the cubs and the fun music?" Together, they rewind to his favorite scene, and she encourages him to listen for how the music changes. "Just like your costume makes you look like a lion, sounds can make us feel different things about the lions," she explains.

Caregivers like Liam's aunt can engage children, even in toddlerhood, with simple questions and observations about the media. Dialoguing with young children about forms of media nurtures awareness that media are constructed with components that can be labeled and categorized (Jolls & Thoman, 2005). Young children can learn to identify a form of media, such as an advertisement within a show, the way they might identify the animals in a farm scene. And they can isolate a component of media production, such as scary or silly music, just as they might identify the foods on their plate. Building on this foundational knowledge, children grow to be able to deconstruct and create messages, becoming more reflective and resilient in their media engagement and less susceptible to advertising, stereotypes, and commercial manipulations encountered across their physical and virtual media ecosystems (Share, 2015).

Because commercial media have unprecedented influence on children's perceptions, attitudes, and behaviors (Linn, 2022), early cultivation of critical media literacy is increasingly essential. Critical media literacy engagement in early childhood helps children grow habits of inquiry and independent and creative expression in complex and exploitative media environments. Critical media practices address both the delights and demands of technologically mediated family life, fostering open communication, co-investigation, informed decision-making, and collaborative problem-solving around the content, use, and impacts of media.

Critical media literacy can support, and even improve, healthy family functioning in the digital age. It empowers individuals of all ages to cultivate self-efficacy and critical autonomy, to embrace intergenerational learning, and to confidently negotiate media influences over time. By embracing the power found in creating and sharing their own stories and by assessing media content for accuracy, bias, and impact, family members take control of their media experiences and relationships and make choices that prioritize collective interests, well-being, and values (see Chapter 5).

The Role of Early Childhood Practitioners. Early childhood practitioners serve as respected sources of expertise for children and families, a role that is both a privilege and a responsibility. Critical media literacy offers applicable concepts and skills to inform their decision-making about whether, how, and why to use screen media within learning environments, and lays the groundwork for informed, ethical, reflective, and socially conscious media engagement.

Media literacy education, like alphabetic literacy, is strengthened by early introduction and immersion, exploring age-appropriate questions and building understandings related to the mediated culture young children experience. Media literacy practices help children learn *how* to think, not *what* to think (Rogow, 2022). Early development of media literacy abilities helps children develop increasingly nuanced understandings over time—growing their understandings of media impacts on society, on learning environments, and on their own lives, and generating their own questions and ideas regarding media texts (Share, 2015).

At the annual book fair, Jackson, a third-grade teacher, notices boys crowding around shelves of books of comics and gross-out science facts, while girls gravitate toward tables loaded with sparkly diaries and fictional chapter books. Before they leave, Jackson gathers the class and encourages them to look around, asking, "What do you notice about how things are set up in here?"

"A lot of the stuff isn't actually books," Miles says. "It feels like there's 'boys' sections and 'girls' sections," adds Lila. As the discussion grows, some wonder if the setup could make kids feel like there were things they should or should not be interested in. Others confess having impulsively spent money on posters and trinkets instead of books. Building on their insights, Jackson says, "What if we look into why the fair is organized like this and how it could be different?"

For over a month, the students explore how products are marketed to kids, including documenting what they notice in local businesses. They brainstorm alternatives for the fair, like organizing books by themes—adventure, animals, and mysteries—and come up with the idea of a "Student Picks" section for kids to share recommendations for other kids. When they present their findings to the principal, they also suggest having fewer nonbook items to encourage more intentional spending.

Through this project, the students develop and practice critical media literacy skills, gaining a deeper understanding of how they can advocate for themselves and create positive change in their learning community. By incorporating early media literacy practices, early childhood practitioners can help young children begin to understand the role of media, including for-profit media, building a foundation for them to "become creative and healthy consumers and creators of media throughout their lives" (Herdzina & Lauricella, 2020, p. 7).

Screen-Aware Protective Factor 5: Resources for Empowerment

Becoming stronger and more confident in managing one's life is gained by having the knowledge, confidence, means, or ability to make decisions for oneself and achieve goals. Young children who are supported by knowledgeable and caring adults build habits for resilience and wellness. Families that have access to relevant information and responsive support can help children navigate their screenscapes. And practitioners who build screen-aware knowledge and practices can model and promote them.

Screen-aware knowledge and resources are empowering. They reduce confusion and helplessness and increase personal agency and confidence. This book compiles screen-aware information, effective practices, and resources for easy access and application. One such resource is the Applying SAFEC tool shown in Figure 4.1. Intended to aid in weighing decisions about whether and how to use screen-based devices and media, it identifies key elements for each guiding principle of the Screen-Aware Framework for Early Childhood that will help determine whether a choice, action, or activity is desirable for use with children. We encourage you to use the Applying SAFEC tool in your work with young children until these considerations

Figure 4.1. Applying the Screen-Aware Framework for Early Childhood (SAFEC)

Is this choice, action, or activity **developmental?**

- ☐ Promotes human interaction and connection
- ☐ Supports growth of executive function and self-regulation
- ☐ Prioritizes child-driven play, imagination, and exploration
- ☐ Allows for experimentation and discovery
- ☐ Preserves opportunities for rest and reflection
- ☐ Contributes to a supportive and enriching environment

Is this choice, action, or activity **researched?**

- ☐ Integrates knowledge of potential risks and harms
- ☐ Includes benefits based on credible research methods and publications
- ☐ Aligns with practice and policy recommendations of professional associations
- ☐ Avoids explicit or implicit perpetuation of common myths and misconceptions related to children and screens
- ☐ Considers the 7 Cs for digital media decision-making: Context, Content, Child, Connections, Calm, Crowding Out, Communication

Is this choice, action, or activity **protective?**

- ☐ Ensures emotional and physical security
- ☐ Builds on individual strengths and promotes protective factors
- ☐ Cultivates critical thinking, autonomy, and resilience
- ☐ Promotes children's rights, including children's right to privacy and right to flourish in digital and online environments
- ☐ Guards against digital online risks for children: Content, Contact, Conduct, Contract, and Commercial

Is this choice, action, or activity **relational**?

- ☐ Avoids screen traps and barriers: technoference, technovoidance, outsourcing, displacement, and trust erosion
- ☐ Sustains connection, trust, and responsiveness between children and caregivers
- ☐ Generates shared media engagement, communication, and discovery
- ☐ Promotes integrated understanding and contextualized experiences (what, why, how)

become second nature to you. More examples of how to use the Applying SAFEC tool appear in Part II of this book.

QUESTIONS FOR REFLECTION

1. How does focusing on strengths rather than deficits make sense to you?
2. Which Screen-Aware Protective Factors can you identify in your own life? Are there any that are missing?
3. How will knowledge of the five Screen-Aware Protective Factors contribute to your professional development and/or practices?
4. How do you envision using the Applying SAFEC tool in your work with young children?

ADVANCING SCREEN AWARENESS

In Part II, we identify priorities, skills, and practical strategies for promoting screen-aware protective factors and mitigating screen-related harms. Chapters focus on fortifying caregiver–child relationships, safeguarding children, and building screen awareness through practices, policies, and partnerships. Each chapter in Part II ends with a brief scenario describing a situation facing an early childhood practitioner who wants to implement screen-aware practices. We hope these "Applying Screen Awareness" scenarios will help you consider how you would respond in similar situations using the information, strategies, and resources described throughout this book.

Part II includes many resource recommendations for prioritizing healthy child development in a screen-saturated world. Foremost among these is the Screen Aware Early Childhood Action Kit, a free, practical, and helpful tool, created in response to feedback from practitioners seeking research-based education and advocacy materials that are printable and easy to use and distribute. Available in English and Spanish, the Action Kit provides

- a ready way to share the topics you've learned about in this book with families, colleagues, and administrators;
- strategies for managing screen use (for children and adults); and
- resources for promoting screen awareness at home and in the classroom.

It includes reproducible Fact and Action Sheets on key topics:

- Learning and Development
- Impacts
- Relationships and Technoference
- Advertising and Media Literacy

- Outdoor Time and Nature
- Screen-Aware Practices for the Home
- Screen-Aware Practices for the Early Childhood Classroom
- Digital Privacy at Home
- Classroom Privacy for Families
- Classroom Privacy for Professionals

Throughout Part II, we reference the Screen Aware Early Childhood Action Kit, which can be found here: https://fairplayforkids.org/pf/eckit/. We encourage you to deepen screen awareness through considering, implementing, and promoting Action Kit resources and advancing the priorities and practices highlighted in the chapters that follow.

Figure II.1. Screen Aware Action Kit Resource for Designating Tech-Free Environments

This sign and other resources are available for download on the TCP website at https://www.tcpress.com/screen-aware-early-childhood-9780807787281, under the "Downloads" tab. Readers will also find additional downloadables, including a sign designating a "phone-free" zone and a flier regarding screen-aware early childhood practice.

CHAPTER 5

Fortifying Caregiver–Child Relationships

The word "screen" has multiple meanings. As a noun, a screen can be a cover or disguise that hides something from view. As a verb, screening can be a way of examining and filtering. In this chapter, we consider the many ways that screen use might cover, hide, or suppress feelings and responses that children and caregivers would otherwise be able to express. We also review how screen use and online behaviors can filter the time, attention, and sensitivity of caring adults. And we share priorities and strategies for strengthening essential connections between caregivers and children.

BARRIERS TO CONNECTION

Attachment theory pioneer John Bowlby described child–caregiver bonds as being as essential as vitamins for physical health, and the child's hunger for them as great as that for food (Bowlby, 1969). Disruption in caregivers' responsiveness and sensitivity can impact children's emotions and behavior and threaten attachment bonds. Understanding and addressing screen technology's impact on caregiving relationships is a critical and consequential component of screen awareness.

Technoference and Technovoidance

Technoference, the groundbreaking term introduced by researchers Brandon McDaniel and Sarah Coyne (2016), describes the everyday interruptions in interpersonal interactions or time together that occur due to digital devices. Technovoidance—a related, yet distinct term coined by child psychologist Dillon Browne (2018)—is defined as "the management and avoidance of unpleasant psychological and physiological states through media and devices" (n.p.). We have discovered that these concepts resonate deeply with practitioners and parents. Adults who care for and educate young children are eager to embrace language that describes their observations and experiences so poignantly and succinctly. Both terms offer helpful framing for understanding and addressing phenomena, such as those described below, that disrupt vital caregiver–child relations.

Diminished Responsiveness. Young children are profoundly dependent on reciprocity with caregivers. Observational data indicate that adult screen use diminishes responsiveness to young children's bids for attention, help, or praise and that when using phones, caregivers frequently disregard children's attempts to interact, sometimes to the extent of neglecting children's safety and emotional needs (Elias et al., 2021).

Compelling evidence exists of the impacts of technoference on adult responsiveness. Studies of caregiver/child dyads in natural settings, like playgrounds, restaurants, and waiting rooms, have shown that when caregivers are using smartphones they are much more likely to delay responding to children, not respond at all, or respond with irritation or in a noncontingent way (Elias et al., 2021; Hiniker et al., 2015; Radesky et al., 2014). Notably, caregivers demonstrate less affect, infrequent to no eye contact, and disengaged body language when on mobile phones and are less responsive when using smartphones than when engaged in other non-child-focused activities such as eating, sipping coffee, or looking at a magazine (Abels et al., 2018; Elias et al., 2021). One study of parents with children ranging in age from 0 to 5 found parents were five times less likely to respond to their child's attempts to get their attention when they were using a phone compared to when they were not (Vanden Abeele et al., 2020).

Researchers note significant increases in safety concerns, instances "when parents did not notice the potential or actual risk to their children's health and safety," and in emotional concerns, instances "when parents ignored their children's attempts to interact, disregarded the children's feelings such as stress or frustration, and/or did not share their children's positive emotions of happiness and accomplishment" associated with prolonged phone use by parents (Elias et al., 2021, p. 380). Caregivers have also believed themselves to be faster and more frequent in responding to their children while using their phones than they actually were (Hiniker et al., 2015), suggesting added risk.

Compromised Relationships. Researchers have begun to look more closely at the impact of screen technologies on the relationship quality of caregivers and young children. Research also considers the bidirectionality of these relations, or the ways in which the characteristics, activities, and behaviors of caregivers and children impact one another—for example, the interplay among screen use, child behavior, and caregiver stress or the impact of nonverbal messages, intended or unintended, that are conveyed when either the caregiver or the child is distracted by screens and ignores the other. These patterns create barriers to connection for both children and adults.

Data collected from child interviews reveal frequent use of words such as "lonely, sad, and angry" when describing time with parents when devices were in use (McDaniel, 2019, p. 75). Parents report feeling anger toward children when children interrupt their phone use and describe children as "less relaxed, more upset, or unsatisfied when the parent is using a device." They report greater problem behaviors when more technological interruptions occur in interactions with their children, and note that family happiness often increases when they put their phone away during family time (McDaniel, 2019, p. 75).

Disrupted Self-Regulation. As the description of technovoidance indicates, individuals of all ages may use screens as a way to avoid or cope with stress and negative emotions—behavior that can have significant implications for self-regulation, the bidirectional benefits (e.g., co-regulation) of caregiver–child interactions, and the overall well-being of young children. For example, research has found that when children exhibit challenging behaviors, parents may turn to technology as a distraction to manage their stress; however, parental reliance on devices can exacerbate the child behaviors that cause the stress, creating cycles of discordance and disruption in the relationship (McDaniel & Radesky, 2018).

Technovoidance is also evident when adults use devices to calm children. Studies have found that children with more challenging temperaments or weaker executive functioning are more likely to be given mobile devices as a soothing tool (Danet et al., 2022; Radesky et al., 2016). While this may provide short-term relief, it can have long-term consequences for children's ability to manage impulses, feelings, and stress. When parents rely on technology for calming, they prevent children from learning to manage their emotions independently, a critical aspect of child development that can have implications in adolescence and beyond.

While technology can serve as a temporary coping mechanism for both caregivers and children, overreliance can interfere with the healthy management of emotions, the development of self-regulation, and the quality and quantity of parent–child interactions. We encourage early childhood practitioners to be aware of these dynamics and consider ways to champion alternative strategies, including the recommendations offered in this chapter and in Fact and Action Sheet #3 in the Screen Aware Early Childhood Action Kit, for reducing technoference and strengthening connections and relationships.

Problematic Media Use

When it comes to protecting children and families from problematic media use (i.e., excessive media use that interferes with normative functioning, as described in Chapter 3), we can look to a systematic review of 35 studies focused on children age 10 and younger designed in part to identify protective factors that could reduce children's problematic media use. Strong parent–child relationships were found to reduce the likelihood of young children of interaction, it still undermines the time that parents and children could spend together.

When adults rely on screen technologies to serve in the place of parenting or educational tasks (i.e., outsource), screen use can get in the way of meaningful relationships and learning. Parents report multiple situations where they permit screen use to help manage their children's behavior. A national survey conducted in 2024 of parents of children ages birth through 8 in the United States found that 47% report using screens to reward good behavior, 44% use screens to keep their child occupied in public settings, and 25% give children screen-based devices to help them calm down when feeling angry, sad, or upset (Mann et al., 2025). Caregiving duties can be tedious and exhausting, but many meaningful opportunities for connection are lost when screens are used for calming or soothing children, motivating routines (such as bedtime), managing behavior, or keeping children occupied during meals, car rides, and errands.

Outsourcing activities to digital tools in early childhood education settings reduces educator–child interactions, compromising the quality of adult–child connections and instructional engagement. Notably, studies show that use of interactive features in digital picture books reduces dialogue between children and teachers (see Undheim, 2022), and that utilizing prompts from electronic books may not be as effective in teaching preschoolers as those provided by adults (Strouse & Ganea, 2016).

STRENGTHENING CONNECTIONS

Strong caregiver–child bonds ensure that children feel supported and understood, fostering connectedness, skills, and resilience for healthy functioning over time. Young children depend on adult attentiveness, responsiveness, and guidance for safety, security, and confidence to thrive in both physical and virtual environments. The following practices promote robust caregiver–child connections and relationships.

Proximal Reciprocity

Proximal reciprocity refers to mutually responsive behaviors and interactions occurring in close physical or emotional proximity. Proximal reciprocity is crucial in fostering and fortifying positive caregiver–child relations, especially in the context of technology use. The good news is that genuinely responsive relationships can withstand short bursts of diminished responsiveness, such as technoference, without lasting damage. Sometimes an adult must respond to an email or text or check their phone. For example, a caregiver can tell a child, "I have to write a quick answer to this email that will take me a couple of minutes, and then I'll be able to fully focus on listening to you." While the child may still be impatient during the time it takes to write the email, when trust and responsiveness have been established the child will know that the caregiver will soon reengage with them.

Similarly, adults can work to avoid technoference in their interactions with other adults. For example, a no-phones policy during drop-off and pickup times in schools and child care centers can encourage educator–family engagement and help families to connect with one another, building relationships and community (see sign resource in Appendix B).

When using digital technology in early childhood education, it's essential that adults provide proximal support, guidance, and reflection. As when engaging children in a book, when adults point to items, ask questions, make eye contact, check for understanding, and have playful responses, teachers can ensure that children's interactions with technology are meaningful and developmentally appropriate.

> Sara, a prekindergarten teacher, recently received a donation of child-friendly digital cameras and has planned a photo scavenger hunt for a leaf project. Over a week, she has introduced the cameras during large- and small-group times, showing the children how to take, save, and delete photos, as well as how to safely handle and store them. On the day of the scavenger hunt, Sara reminds the children that the classroom cameras are special tools to use for projects. As the children explore, she notices Quinn and Devon giggling as they take close-up pictures of each other's faces. Smiling, Sara sits beside them and says, "I can see you're having fun! Cameras can be great for goofy photos, but today we're using them to capture pictures of our leaf hunt challenges."
>
> She then asks, "Which challenges are left on your list?" Devon eagerly shows the challenges they have checked off their illustrated checklist, and Sara notes, "It looks like you still need to take a picture of a leaf design. Maybe you could make a funny face out of leaves to photograph instead of funny faces of each other?" Inspired, Quinn exclaims, "Yes! Come on! I saw a leaf that can be the tongue!"

By staying close, engaging playfully, and guiding their focus back to the activity, Sara has helped the children use the cameras meaningfully, blending fun with purposeful exploration.

Joint Media Engagement

Joint media engagement is a powerful approach for enhancing caregiver–child relationships, turning screen time and use into opportunities for meaningful interaction. More than co-viewing, joint media engagement involves caregiver and child participation, fostering socially contingent interactions that help transfer learning beyond the screen. Caregivers ask questions, label objects, provide context, and discuss the content displayed on screens, deepening the child's understanding and engagement. For support of a trusted adult as they learn to understand and navigate their screenscapes. Incorporating the questions shown above in your daily practices with young children is a powerful strategy for establishing and building joint media engagement. You may find it helpful to practice asking and answering these questions in your own media encounters first, to increase your media literacy skills and comfort level.

Parental Media Efficacy

Parental self-efficacy refers to a caregiver's confidence in their ability to handle parenting tasks well and guide their child's behavior effectively. Strong self-efficacy is associated with many positive child and parent outcomes and can have a significant impact on lowering problematic media use, technoference, and technovoidance. Longitudinal research finds that early restrictive media monitoring (including setting rules and limits on screen time and content) serves as a protective measure against child problematic media use later on (Coyne et al., 2023). Lower parental self-efficacy, however, has been associated with higher levels of child screen time (Chen et al., 2020) and less frequent parental media monitoring (Shin, 2018). Parents who feel "inefficacious, anxious, or doubtful about their own parenting capability" allow children to have more time on screens (Chen et al., 2020, p. 9).

Parental media monitoring, also known as parental mediation, is employed by parents to reduce their children's overall media exposure and to encourage them to think critically about their media use (Coyne et al., 2023). Parental mediation can take different forms. Restrictive mediation involves setting rules and limits on the amount of time children can spend on media, as well as the type of content they can access. Active mediation refers to direct parent-to-child interaction and conversation about media experiences, uses, content, and effects. Parents also mediate indirectly by cultivating conditions and environments that promote healthy media habits and encounters. Research on parental media efficacy indicates that high levels of restrictive media monitoring are appropriate, and even advantageous, for young children and correlate with healthier child media habits over time (Coyne et al., 2023). As children transition into middle childhood, restrictive mediation is shown to be less impactful than active mediation.

Screen awareness helps make important links between parenting, media use and management, and child outcomes. A 2024 national survey found that a majority of parents of young children in the United States "take a hands-off approach to managing their child's screen time," with 75% not using tools or settings to limit it and 51% not restricting the type of content (Mann et al., 2025, p. 29). Parents of children ages 5 to 8 are much more likely than parents of children younger than 2 to use tools to manage screen time and to restrict content (Mann et al., 2025). In support of adult–child relationships, we encourage you to find ways to promote parental media efficacy and parental mediation. The following recommendations from researchers are a great way to start:

- Empower parents to learn about media impacts and management practices through education and messaging, and by providing resources and assistance where needed.
- Promote parenting resources and education that improve parent–child relationships, bolster parents' confidence and self-belief, increase effective parenting practices, and reduce parental stress.
- Emphasize parental mediation behaviors (e.g., media monitoring, joint media engagement) that have been shown to scaffold young children's healthy media use and behaviors.

(Chen et al., 2020; Coyne et al., 2023; Shin, 2018)

Digital Trust

Adults foster trustful relationships by ensuring children's emotional and physical safety and security across all settings, including digital and virtual realms. Building and maintaining digital trust is an increasingly important dimension of caregiver–child relationships, serving to balance adults' needs and intentions with children's needs and setting the stage for online experiences that are respectful, positive, and secure.

To establish and preserve digital trust, adults can model and maintain thoughtful online engagement. Creating digital trust involves considering who will have access to shared information, the nature of the content, and any potential for unintended consequences, such as how publicly shared content might "haunt or taunt" children in the present and the future (Heitner, 2023). Caregivers can ask themselves: Who will see this? What are the current and future impacts of the content shared? When should permission be asked of children? and How might this content affect the child over time? Building digital trust bolsters caregiver–child relationships, laying foundations that will help children navigate the digital world responsibly and safely.

To promote digital trust, practitioners can grow their awareness of the perils and pitfalls of technoference, technovoidance, and sharenting; model and maintain responsible digital and online stewardship; and ensure informed consent and transparency in digital interactions with children and families.

Strengthening Relationships With Screen Awareness

Encouraging the following daily screen-aware practices, detailed in the Screen Aware Early Childhood Action Kit, can lead to stronger caregiver–child relationships. These practices can be adapted for home, child care, and school settings.

- Introduce daily screen-free times and spaces. Small but concentrated doses of screen-free attention make big impacts!
- Establish and maintain screen media routines and boundaries. Set expectations and let children know of any changes to routines ahead of time.
- Turn off distracting sounds and notifications. Put devices away when not actively using them to reduce unnecessary distractions and interruptions. Screen-based distractions can cause missed cues and bids for attention. Use "do not disturb" or "silent" settings on phones during one-on-one time with children.
- Put down screens when communicating with children. Eye contact and face-to-face interactions let children know they are seen, safe, and connected.
- When screen use is required, let children know what you are doing on your screen and when you will be done. This helps children learn that technology is a tool used for specific purposes and that they are not being ignored.
- Incorporate children's perspectives into screen media boundaries and management, such as parameters for smartphone use.
- Avoid background media—turn it off when not watching or listening. Keep screen media off when children are playing and during daily routines like mealtime, naptime, and bedtime.
- Build screen awareness by sharing children's books such as:
  » *Screens Away, Time to Play* by Kailan Carr
  » *Me, Myselfie & I: A Cautionary Tale* by Jamie Lee Curtis
  » *Connor Crowe Can't Let Go* by Howard Pearlstein
  » *If You Give a Mouse an iPhone* by Ann Droyd
  » *You're Missing It!* by Brady Smith and Tiffani Thiessen
  » *The Glowing Rectangle* by Katie Friedman

Parents and practitioners can also find helpful advice about building and sustaining adult–child relationships and protecting those relationships from the negative impacts of screen use through such organizations as The Durable Human (https://durablehuman.com/) and the Fred Rogers Institute (https://www.fredrogersinstitute.org/).

SUMMARY OF KEY POINTS

- Technoference refers to interruptions in interpersonal interactions due to screen-based devices. Technovoidance refers to using media and devices to manage and avoid unpleasant feelings or psychological states. Use of screen technology in these ways can negatively impact vital caregiver–child relationships.

- Technoference and technovoidance are associated with diminished responsiveness on the part of adults and disrupted self-regulation in young children.
- Posting images and information about children online without their full understanding and consent can be damaging to children's privacy, emotional health, and relationships with caregivers.
- Strong caregiver–child relationships reduce the likelihood of children developing problematic media use.
- Caregivers can promote strong bonds with children through responsiveness and attentiveness. Strategies to mitigate negative impacts of screen media include using joint media engagement skills, teaching critical media literacy, monitoring children's media use by setting guidelines, and building digital trust.

APPLYING SCREEN AWARENESS

Jia has been working in the same child care center for 5 years as an infant and toddler teacher. Her program practices "looping," which means that she stays with the same group of children for 2 years. Jia appreciates having the opportunity to get to know a group of babies and their families well over time.

The six children in her current class range in age from 15 to 22 months. She knows that several families are struggling with screen-related issues, in her class and in the other infant/toddler classes as well. One 18-month-old frequently arrives crying, and the baby's father has told Jia that he allows her to watch videos on his phone in the car but she screams when he takes it away. She has overheard parents and grandparents mention characters from TV shows that the children watch. And one mother has asked Jia if she should be allowing her daughter to watch toddler shows because all her friends' children are.

Jia's program is planning for a Parent Open House event in a few weeks, and Jia would like to offer a short workshop about screen media management for families of infants and toddlers. She is aiming to keep the presentation to half an hour. Jia wants to focus on the importance of parent/child relationships and the ways technology can impact relationships.

1. Of the information presented in this chapter, what are three points Jia could focus on that would be most relevant for families of infants and toddlers? Why do you think these points are significant?
2. How could Jia use the Screen-Aware Framework for Early Childhood to help her prepare the workshop?

CHAPTER 6

Safeguarding Children From Exploitation

It's almost impossible for young children to avoid the powerful influence of advertising and consumerist values. Although other countries such as Norway, Sweden, France, and Germany restrict advertising to children, the United States has no such safeguards in place. This chapter identifies some of the major sources of digital risks and harms for children, including child-targeted advertising, manipulative design techniques, and privacy violations. We underscore the importance of supporting children's right to grow up free of digital exploitation and share priorities for promoting child privacy and child-centered digital design.

CHILDREN AS TARGETS

Once upon a time, advertising spoke primarily to parents, not children. Children's advertising creep began with popular contests, cereal box top rewards, and even advertising in schools, as early as the 1920s. Advertising to children exploded in the early 1950s when most U.S. households introduced televisions, especially as children began watching Saturday morning cartoons. Restrictions on advertising to children existed through the mid-1980s, when the Federal Trade Commission removed them, allowing the marketplace free rein.

In the late 1980s, Congress passed a bill championed by advocate Peggy Charren, president of Action for Children's Television, that would have limited advertising time, eliminated program-length toy and product commercials, and required educational programming. But President Ronald Reagan vetoed the bill, claiming that it violated free speech. Without these restrictions, corporate marketers gained unprecedented access to children's attention, and that access has increased dramatically over time. Advocates and lawmakers are designing and championing legislation to institute protections, but at the time of this publication, none have been established.

Marketers target young children because of the direct influence they have on their parents' spending. An immersive marketing universe, which includes brand licensing, product placement, marketing in schools, and social media influencers, preys on young children. Across media, apps, games, and even educational curricula, corporate brands target children from birth, striving to create "cradle-to-grave" loyalty.

Advertising is baked into everything children see and do online. And because devices are mobile, marketers can have a presence in the stroller, the crib, the car, the grocery cart, the classroom, and other previously ad-free spaces of childhood. Without legislated guardrails, there are ample avenues for brands to be in front of a child's face every waking moment of every day. Nonconsensual exposure to marketing messages is particularly egregious because young children often struggle to distinguish between an ad and the programming itself and are still developing the sophistication to recognize persuasive intent. This chapter provides an inventory of ways that for-profit corporations dominate screenscapes in the United States, violating children's rights to autonomy and commercial-free childhoods.

Branding and Advertising

The current online world is driven by messaging that seduces children into thinking buying equals happiness. Sophisticated marketing techniques and products linked to programming condition children to want more and more. The line is further blurred when advertising is disguised as content. A basically unrestricted marketing industry has largely normalized the following practices, changing the nature of childhood in the 21st century.

Branded Characters and Parasocial Relationships. Parasocial relationships, one-sided relationships children build with media characters, can influence families' purchasing habits and ultimately their values. A child's interest in, or bond with, a fictional character can support attachment, trust, and emotional security. Children think of them as friends. These one-sided relationships can be easily exploited by advertisers to promote unhealthy foods, branded toys, or other media.

Once young children bond with characters, they are more likely to nag parents to buy program-themed toys, clothing, bed linens, backpacks, and countless other items. When brand marketers intentionally commercialize these relationships, the trust and attachment children feel toward popular, often beloved characters is rerouted toward profit-driven ends. Many children's app designs use characters to encourage in-app purchases, even going so far as to make a child feel guilty by having the character cry or whine if the child uses a free option rather than the paid option (Meyer et al., 2019). Since young children cannot recognize overt forms of exploitation, they are more likely to believe that "If I spend money, I'll make my friend happy, and that's good."

Practitioners can help children by keeping character discussions centered on their narratives and positive personality traits and away from the associated products. For instance, avoid overemphasizing a princess t-shirt or a superhero lunch box. If the characters come up in play or conversation, stay away from exclaiming about the branded products.

Hidden Ads and Advergames. Exploiting parasocial relationships is only one of many manipulative techniques or "dark digital design" patterns used to hold children's attention. A 2019 study of 135 apps used by young children found that four out of five featured multiple deceptive practices to keep children engaged and that 95% contained at least one type of advertising. These techniques included: use of commercial characters; full-app teasers; advertising videos either interrupting play as pop-ups or required to unlock play items; in-app purchases; prompts to rate the app or share on social media; and distracting ads such as banners across the screen or hidden ads with misleading symbols such as "$" camouflaged as gameplay items. Free apps displayed significantly more advertising (100% versus 88% of paid apps), but advertising occurred at similar rates in apps labeled as "educational" versus other categories (Meyer et al., 2019).

Advergames—games or apps utilizing brand characters, colors, and images to promote products—can keep children exposed to product ads for hours without them (or their parents) even realizing it. Children can inadvertently become marketers themselves when coaxed to forward links to others (Pauze & Kent, 2021). Most popular in the food and beverage industry, advergames create brand awareness and loyalty by making the logo, colors, and characters prominent, memorable, and fun. For example, one popular game has users, already familiar with the candy characters, try to prevent them from being dropped into hot chocolate. Advergames are often cross-marketed via social media posts to persuade parents to buy both the apps and the product for their children.

Some apps embed ads within the gameplay, meaning that they offer children the opportunity to watch ads to gain more coins or tokens, unlock levels, or get better items (for example, a faster tool that helps them play the game more easily). This leads to children watching many more ads because they want to get ahead in the game.

Practitioners can learn to spot hidden ads and avoid advergames altogether, choosing ad-free apps as needed. When advertising appears prominent, you can point it out to children and share why you have decided not to utilize the app, helping to grow early media literacy.

Kidfluencers. With the advent of social media, influencers—"celebrities" hired to promote products during and around posts about their lives—became popular. Child influencers or "kidfluencers" began appearing in their parents' posts, generating income to those parents as their cute and precocious personalities drove millions in sponsored revenue. The Federal Trade Commission now requires a statement of transparency about the endorsements, but many influencers don't make it obvious, or they find new ways to capitalize on the brand's recognition.

Kidfluencers have also exploded in popularity, further blurring the lines between entertainment and advertising. Companies like Walmart and Mattel have lucrative endorsement deals with families of young children with large followings. As a result, children who are too young to make their own accounts on platforms are still utilized to promote brands and products (Linn, 2022). Often kidfluencers promote products like makeup, handbags, or sports equipment, adult items that contribute to the diminishing of childhood for them and their viewers. Kidfluencers themselves often find that creating a certain image and branding themselves online takes time and value from creative play, real-world relationships, exploring, and just being themselves.

Age Compression

Kidfluencers also blur the boundaries between childhood and teenage culture. If you've ever wondered why children seem like little adults—in their clothing, language, dance moves, and attitudes—welcome to the idea that it's a carefully designed plot by corporate advertisers. Exploitation of a child's natural urge to seem older and more mature is a widely used marketing strategy. Media content, toys, games, and clothing once marketed only to teens and young adults are now pushed on younger and younger children. Descriptors such as *age conflation, boundary ambiguity,* and *KGOY* (for Kids Getting Older Younger) are used to describe the diminishing distinction between different life stages, particularly between childhood and adolescence or adolescence and adulthood.

These concepts also reflect broader societal shifts in attitudes toward childhood, challenging traditional notions of developmental stages and raising questions about the impact of technological changes on children's well-being, identity formation, and socialization processes. When young children work hard to continually imitate older children, they miss developmental foundations essential to being ready for later experiences (Levin, 2013). Practitioners can help children process adult or older content using art, play, and conversation and then redirect their energies to developmentally appropriate play. We encourage practitioners to express interest in children's online lives and keep alert to the techniques described in this chapter, which, when encountered regularly, push children to rush through childhood.

Sexualization. Graphic images about sex and being sexy assault young children through devices, apps, and screens in public places like stores, restaurants, and billboards. Entertainment, toy, and clothing industries, to name a few, profit from sexualized messaging that can be confusing and even frightening for young children. They learn to associate the "right" physical appearance with popularity and belonging. The sexualization of childhood encourages treating oneself and others as objects of desire, primarily related to physical attractiveness (Levin & Kilbourne, 2009).

Repeated exposure to sexual imagery compromises children's age-appropriate development of understandings of intimacy and relationships. With awareness of rampant sexualization in the media and advertising, practitioners can learn what children are seeing and hearing in their media, help them process the images and messages, and gently guide them through books and real-life examples to healthy, developmentally appropriate messages about intimate relationships and body image.

Violence. Similarly, the entertainment industry markets increasingly more realistic violence to young children, which can impact attitudes and behavior and be traumatizing. Film and video game industries target children as young as preschool age with toy tie-ins for adult-rated movies and games. Superhero movies rated PG-13 spawn products from toddler Halloween costumes to sleeping bags and lunch boxes designed for young children, indoctrinating them to franchises early and often. Children can easily join active multiplayer video games, increasing exposure to adult content, predators, bullying, racism, hate speech, and extremism (Harriman et al., 2020). And many young children witness violence in the news media through exposure in home and public settings. The American Academy of Pediatrics Council on Communications and Media (2016b) has issued statements on the impact of virtual violence on children, cautioning that immersion into media violence causes children to be desensitized to real-life violence and that children exposed to violent media at a young age become more aggressive later in life.

It may seem, then, that violent play should be discouraged. It's not that simple. Ideally, children would not be exposed in the first place; however, when they do encounter violent media, it will often be revealed in their conversations and play, presenting important opportunities for adult engagement and guidance. When children merely imitate media scripts, they are not processing the violence they have seen. But free play provides opportunities for them to re-create scenes in ways that incorporate new dimensions and outcomes stemming from their own imaginations, allowing them to have a sense of industry, ownership, and safety. Children use their play to work through their experiences and build new understandings. Within a safe setting, acting out violence in play is not always a bad thing (Levin & Carlsson-Paige, 2006).

Practitioners can talk with children to understand what media images they have experienced, what individual meaning they are making of the experience, and what strong feelings might be leading to aggressive behavior. Despite the mass marketing of violence, each child incorporates it differently and will have different sensitivities, responses, and coping strategies.

Problematic Digital Design

Young children are developmentally unable to distinguish persuasive intent in advertising until the ages of 5–7. Digital design allows for levels of manipulation that remain imperceptible to children (and even adolescents and adults). Many companies employ psychological expertise to embed advertising and keep children engaged in the app or program, in ways that exploit children's developmental vulnerabilities. These practices are known as *persuasive design.*

When a small child plays with a ball, she might play for a while and then move on to getting a snack, snuggling with a parent, or petting her cat. But when she is playing on a tablet or phone, the app or game is likely employing techniques designed to override all other curiosities in her environment and even her basic bodily needs. Features that use psychological, physical, and/or social manipulation to keep children scrolling are employing a range of persuasive design techniques, as detailed in Table 6.1. Familiarizing yourself with these techniques can help you anticipate children's responses and steer clear of apps, platforms, and games that employ them.

Many apps that claim to be educational utilize the design manipulations listed above. Practitioners can begin by investigating educational claims on apps, games, or programs. Check whether the research cited is conducted by independent sources or by the company that designed the app. Practitioners can establish a policy of using only ad-free screen content or limiting screen use in order to reduce exposure to manipulative design. Fact and Action Sheet #4 in the Screen Aware Early Childhood Action Kit, which focuses on Advertising and Media Literacy, can be a useful resource for practitioners and families.

CHILD RIGHTS AND RISKS IN THE DIGITAL AGE

The United Nations Convention on the Rights of the Child (1989) establishes the child rights of provision, protection, and participation, guidance that can be applied to children's rights online, where risks are often amplified. As families with young children navigate the screenscape and young children gain access to the Internet and Internet-enabled devices, the safely and protections they deserve offline also apply to their online and digital experiences. Children's rights to privacy and to protection from sexual and aggressive threats, discrimination, violence, abuse, exploitation, and neglect all apply in virtual realms. Rights to freedom of information, expression, and agency apply as well. A rights framework encourages us to look at every child's unique journey as shaped by provisions and protections of their offline environments and their online environments, where similar protections do not yet exist (Livingstone, 2016).

Table 6.1. Exploitation in Children's Digital Experience Design

	Exploitation in Children's Digital Experience Design
Psychological Manipulation	**Confirm-Shaming/Guilt:** App design that shames children, making them feel they have done something wrong if they do not make in-app purchases.
	Reciprocity: Game or app that requires children to watch ads in order to get tokens or game play items.
	Time-Based Pressure: Designs that reduce user autonomy to pause or end play; visual indicators such as countdown timers convey that time is running out, which interferes with decision-making and promotes purchasing quickly and continuing to the next level.
	Freemiums: Children are offered a basic app or game for free, which comes with limited access. Completing the game or accessing special features costs money.
	Gamification: The application of game-design elements in nongame contexts to captivate children with elements such as badges, points, levels, and other adrenaline-raising persuasive elements.
Physical Manipulation	**Dopamine reward activation:** Game and app features that stimulate children's brains to produce dopamine, a chemical neurotransmitter that rewards certain behaviors and motivates children to repeat them.
	Interference: Using a style and visual presentation to steer users to or away from certain choices.
	Pacing: Fast-moving frames, often accompanied by loud and fast sounds, which create confusion and can exacerbate attention problems.
Social Manipulation	**Undisclosed Influencers:** Children promoting brands to other children without proper sponsorship disclosures.
	Popularity Metrics: Numbers associated with users' engagement that are displayed prominently in a profile or post.
	FOMO: Fear of missing out; using content that expires or disappears.
Other Deceptive Practices	**Forced Actions:** Coercing players into doing something tangential to complete their task, such as sharing personal information.
	AutoPlay: Algorithm that feeds a new video as soon as one is finished, designed to keep children's attention longer and serve more ads.
	Infinite Scroll: Content feeds that load automatically without an end point or requiring initiation by the user.

(continued)

Table 6.1. (*continued*)

> **Seamless Payments:** Design that removes steps or barriers to payment, like one-click options.
>
> **Nagging:** A child cannot play unless an unrelated action is performed, such as clicking on a link or downloading.
>
> **Kidified Content:** Using popular cartoon or fictional figures to get children to watch adult content.

Sources: Bessant et al., 2023; Everyschool, 2022; Radesky et al., 2022.

Notes: 1. This is not an exhaustive list of children's app manipulations, but provides an overview of the most prominent ones. 2. Children in low-socioeconomic families encounter manipulative design features more often. Exploratory evidence builds upon existing research on inequities in child access to quality media by demonstrating an uneven prevalence of manipulative designs intended to monetize children's online experiences (Radesky et al., 2022).

Online Risks

Promoting child well-being in the digital age requires identifying and respecting children's rights, both offline and online. It also necessitates awareness of risks and harms across physical and virtual ecosystems. Online risks and harms, in particular, present distinctive challenges for research, policy, and practice due to a wide range of variables and exacerbating or mitigating impacts. To begin, it helps to differentiate between risks and harms—*risk* being the chance of harm occurring, and *harm* involving actual negative impacts on a child's emotional, physical, or mental well-being and the interplay of variables that impact outcomes (Livingstone & Stoilova, 2021).

> *Five-year-old Xavier, unnoticed by his father, who is packing his snack for school, starts watching a violent movie trailer that plays immediately following the video his dad gave him permission to watch. Xavier's little brother plops next to him on the couch, trying to join in. Annoyed by the disruption, Xavier impulsively enacts one of the moves he just saw on the screen, pinning his brother to the floor and hurting his arm (and feelings) in the process. Xavier's dad intervenes, angrily sending Xavier to wait in the car until it's time to leave.*
>
> *Distracted by responding to an injured and upset toddler, Xavier's dad says nothing to him except a brief warning to behave when leaving Xavier at the school door. Xavier enters the classroom feeling dejected and agitated. His teacher notices that he does not seem like himself when he does not join Amir at the magnet area, his usual routine, choosing to sit and watch out the window instead.*
>
> *Xavier's buddy Amir had also encountered the very same movie trailer streaming on a grouping of televisions in the electronics section of a store while running an errand with his grandfather. Noticing that the fighting and explosions on the screen had*

captured Amir's attention, his grandfather guided him away and toward the items on their list.

On the bus ride home Amir's grandfather revisited their encounter with the movie trailer, reminding him that special effects were used to make it and that people in real life would be hurt much more than the characters were on the screen if the same thing happened to them. Amir told his grandpa that he plans to watch that movie when he is old enough. His grandpa asked if he will remember what he told him about special effects and acting. Amir nodded a quick yes before pointing out the new machine at the construction site that they had noticed on the way to the store.

Although both Xavier and Amir were exposed to the same violent media, the difference in their outcomes highlights the varying impacts of digital risks. Xavier, watching alone, reacted impulsively, imitating the violent behavior he saw on the screen. His developmental inability to process the content appropriately and the absence of adult guidance led to harm for his little brother and emotional distress and disconnection for himself. In contrast, the attentive and protective interventions applied by his grandfather helped Amir navigate a moment of risk, reducing the likelihood of harmful outcomes. As discussed throughout this book, and exemplified by Xavier and Amir, digital risks and opportunities need to be considered within the bioecological circumstances of the child. Each child's experience varies based on factors like age, gender, media literacy, parental efficacy, family background, and the bidirectional impacts of their larger developmental ecology (e.g., meso-, macro-, and chronosystems).

New risks and harms emerge as screenscapes evolve, often faster than adults can develop strategies to address them. Effectively addressing online risks, however, requires avoiding assumptions and/or anxiety and using approaches grounded in research. It also includes understanding how the design and management of digital environments impact child outcomes (Livingstone & Stoilova, 2021).

Online risk classifications have been widely incorporated as a point of reference for identifying and assessing sociotechnical landscapes and policy interventions. The classifications of online risk have been refined over time, most recently through collaboration between EU Kids Online and the Children Online: Research and Evidence (CO:RE) consortium (see Livingstone & Stoilova, 2021). The CO:RE 4Cs classification identifies that online risks arise when a child:

- engages with and/or is exposed to potentially harmful **CONTENT;**
- experiences and/or is targeted by potentially harmful **CONTACT;**
- witnesses, participates in, and/or is a victim of potentially harmful **CONDUCT;** and/or
- is party to and/or exploited by a potentially harmful **CONTRACT.**
(Livingstone & Stoilova, 2021)

While we hope for a day when young children are free of these risks, many current social, ecological, and digital conditions exacerbate them instead. The CO:RE 4 Cs classification outlines two dimensions of online risk: the child's positioning in relation to the digital world (i.e., content, contact, conduct, contract) and the type of risk they face (i.e., aggressive, sexual, values; Livingstone & Stoilova, 2021). It also includes cross-cutting risks like threats to children's privacy, health, and fair treatment. These risks can occur in relation to any type of content, contact, conduct, or contract online. The classification recognizes that online risks often overlap and become more complex as the digital exposure increases. The CO:RE classification presented in Table 6.2 details potential risks and serves as a cautionary reminder of children's need for protection in online environments.

"Smart" Toys and the Internet of Things. The Internet of Things refers to wireless online connections and sensors embedded in everyday household items—appliances, thermostats, doorbells—and children's playthings, often categorized as "smart" toys. Children perceive smart toys as fun, enjoying their humanlike qualities and personalized responses. Parents and grandparents buy connected toys because they are novel and engaging, often with the belief that they might offer a learning benefit. In violation of the Children's Online Privacy and Protection Act (COPPA) (see Chapter 8), undisclosed surveillance capabilities (e.g., recording of conversations and sensitive information) are present in many Wi-Fi–enabled toys, introducing significant privacy risks (Brito et al., 2018).

In 2015, advocates at Fairplay (then the Campaign for a Commercial-Free Childhood) launched a public education campaign about the dangers of Mattel's Wi-Fi–enabled Hello Barbie doll, which recorded children's private conversations, transmitted them to cloud servers that analyzed them by algorithms, and shared the data with Mattel employees and third parties. The doll asked the child many questions like "What's your middle name?" and "What's your favorite restaurant?" The doll then replied with content tailored to the child's family, experiences, likes, and dislikes. Due to the campaign, the Hello Barbie product flopped in the market (Fairplay, 2015). Yet similar Wi-Fi–enabled toys are still very popular.

Edtech. Educational technology (edtech), which introduces hardware, software, and online tools into curriculum, starts as early as preschool. Edtech companies capitalized on the need for virtual classrooms during the COVID-19 pandemic, growing in reach (and profit). Estimates of prepandemic annual spending on K–12 edtech in the United States were between $26 billion and $41 billion, and the market is expected to grow to over $132 billion by 2032 (Shinde, 2024). When used uncritically, edtech can displace essential relationships with teachers who scaffold learning and can get in the way of real-world socialization with other students.

Edtech systems are often used for testing and assessments. Children as young as kindergarten may be required to complete assessments online,

Table 6.2. The CO:RE Classification of Online Risk to Children

ONLINE RISKS	CONTENT *Child engages with or is exposed to potentially harmful content*	CONTACT *Child experiences or is targeted by potentially harmful adult contact*	CONDUCT *Child witnesses, participates in, or is a victim of potentially harmful peer conduct*	CONTRACT *Child is party to or exploited by potentially harmful contract*
AGGRESSIVE	Violent, gory, graphic racist, hateful, or extremist information and communication	Harassment, stalking, hateful behavior, unwanted or excessive surveillance	Bullying, hateful or hostile communication, or peer activity such as trolling, exclusion, shaming	Identity theft, fraud, phishing, scams, hacking, blackmail, security risks
SEXUAL	Pornography (harmful or illegal), sexualization of culture, oppressive body image norms	Sexual harassment, sexual grooming, sextortion, the generation and sharing of child sexual abuse material	Sexual harassment, nonconsensual sexual messaging, adverse sexual pressures	Trafficking for purposes of sexual exploitation, streaming (paid-for) child sexual abuse
VALUES	Mis/disinformation, age-inappropriate marketing, or user-generated content	Ideological persuasion or manipulation, radicalization, and extremist recruitment	Potentially harmful user communities, e.g., self-harm, adverse peer pressures	Gambling, hyper-personalized recommendations that create isolation (i.e., filter bubbles), microtargeting, dark patterns shaping persuasion or purchase
CROSS-CUTTING	**Privacy violations** (interpersonal, institutional, commercial) **Physical and mental health risks** (e.g., sedentary lifestyle, excessive screen use, isolation, anxiety) **Inequalities and discrimination** (in/exclusion, exploiting vulnerability, algorithmic bias, predictive analytics)			

Adapted from Livingstone & Stoilova, 2021.

even though they may not have the fine-motor capability to use the keyboard or touchscreen. This forces kindergarten teachers to adjust their curriculum to include teaching children the skills they will need simply to respond to assessment questions.

Some edtech platforms engage in social profiling of children to manipulate their behavior, resulting in risks of discrimination. Popular classroom management and communication software uses points-based systems as a kind of social scoring. The software allows teachers to publicly share the behavior-based points scored by children in the class on a whiteboard and/ or with families, which can lead to shame, humiliation, and misunderstanding (Hooper et al., 2022).

Programs provided for "free" come with a hidden price, including the collection and extrapolation of data. Surveillance and profiling of children's data for commercial purposes emerges in many edtech tools. Lengthy and complex privacy policies make it nearly impossible for educators or administrators to understand the intent or determine compliance with children's privacy legislation, yet schools and school districts are held legally accountable for allowing use without ensuring that legal standards are met (Atabey & Hooper, 2024). In the United States, the Federal Trade Commission has issued a policy statement emphasizing that children should not be subject to edtech surveillance as a condition of accessing educational tools and that teachers and parents should not be forced to accept these practices (Atabey & Hooper, 2024).

Although some forms of educational technology can be useful, teacher-led instruction is most likely to promote student learning (Everyschool, 2022). Practitioners can ensure that screens are employed for specific learning purposes not available in other forms. They can also choose technology that can be shared by large groups and small groups, guided by the teacher, and used for specific outcomes.

The Right to Digital Privacy

Digital privacy violations generate risks and harms for young children, their families, and early childhood practitioners. The increasing "datafication" of childhood—where children's actions, behaviors, and even physical attributes are turned into digital data—poses significant risks to their rights and well-being. This process reduces children to data points within algorithms, stripping away their individuality and subjecting them to potential harms that they, their parents, and educators cannot fully understand or control (Siibak & Mascheroni, 2021). The implications of such practices are far-reaching, affecting not only children's current experiences but also their self-image, social relations, opportunities, and personal rights and autonomy over time.

Researchers identify three categories of privacy risks affecting children: interpersonal, commercial, and institutional. Interpersonal breaches result from the data practices of their families and other known relations (e.g., sharenting); commercial breaches happen when children's activities, behaviors, and bodies (e.g., location, biometric data) are tracked through different apps and monitoring devices; and institutional breaches are largely associated with schools and other child-serving establishments that utilize data-driven technologies (Livingstone & Stoilova, 2021).

Priorities for Children and Families. Data collected on children fails to represent the full complexity of their lives. This reductive and deeply problematic practice can lock children into narrow data profiles known to perpetuate stereotypes and biases, including racial and gender prejudices, among others (Linn, 2022).

> *Hector and Maria, 7-year-old twins, love watching TV together, especially cooking shows. Excited about their family's new streaming service, their 12-year-old sister, Ana, creates a profile for each of them, ensuring that they are set to the highest levels of protection and privacy, as their mom has insisted. The three siblings have fun loading the streaming service to their personal tablets and choosing screen names and images.*
>
> *Hector, recently curious about jungles, is thrilled when a safari adventure show is recommended in his listings for "boys." Meanwhile, Maria's screen fills with suggestions labeled for "girls," many featuring princesses and adorable animated animals. As the weeks go by, Hector and Maria find it harder to enjoy the same programs, and their shared viewing time dwindles. Hector becomes absorbed in his action-packed shows, while Maria gravitates toward stories filled with magic and friendship. Hector tries to look for a children's cooking program that he saw on Maria's tablet, but after scrolling as far as possible on his options and listings, he never can find it.*

The story of Hector and Maria provides a glimpse into how data-driven decisions within apps, video streaming services, and educational software can influence the content children see, shaping their preferences and behaviors in ways that might not align with their true interests, capacities, or developmental needs. These practices raise serious concerns about children's autonomy, as they are often unable to consent to or comprehend the ways in which they are being tracked and profiled.

Families are also affected by the pervasive collection of data. Modern parenting is increasingly intertwined with digital technologies that encourage constant monitoring and surveillance of children under the guise of care. This practice, sometimes referred to as "babyveillance," pressures parents to engage in intensive monitoring of their children's safety and well-being. From pregnancy apps that track fetal development, to baby tech gadgets that monitor newborns, to wristwatches for children that allow parents (and companies) to track them, to the normalization of sharenting on social media discussed in Chapter 5, parents are drawn into cycles of surveillance designed to feed a data-driven business model known as *surveillance capitalism* (Siibak & Mascheroni, 2021).

Surveillance capitalism exploits the parental need to protect and care for their children, turning their parenting practices into data-driven opportunities for profit. Although these tools promise peace of mind and stronger connections, they often strain family dynamics by heightening parental anxiety and turning the private aspects of family life into marketable commodities.

When everything from toys to baby monitors can be connected to the Internet, it can be challenging to maintain children's privacy. Many early childhood programs and services incorporate home visits and regularly share resources for parents to incorporate at home. Promoting the home privacy tips in Table 6.3 can be a great way to build awareness.

Priorities for Practitioners. As digital technologies become more embedded in early learning settings, educators may find themselves engaging with digital tools and platforms that collect and analyze data on staff and students. This can create ethical dilemmas and complicate the protection of children's privacy and well-being. Pressure to use data-driven tools in early elementary classrooms without adequate training and support can contribute to digital data risks while shifting time and focus away from holistic, child-centered approaches to education. Early childhood programs that use digital devices have an obligation to protect the personal information of children and families. Integration of the privacy principles and practices shown in Table 6.4 will provide a strong foundation.

You can also support young children and their families through modeling and raising awareness of the right to privacy across early learning environments using strategies such as the following:

- Consider whether use is necessary prior to adopting online programs and/or applications.
- Restrict use of personal devices for classroom practices.
- Create, communicate, and maintain policies for taking and sharing pictures and videos (see Chapter 8).
- Limit child documentation so as not to distract children or disrupt interactions and activities.
- Restrict use of social media for family, classroom, or program communications.
- Provide notification and obtain parental permission before using any edtech app or website that collects information from children (and adhere to all relevant program or school policies related to data privacy).

For these and additional ideas, see Fact and Action Sheet #10, Classroom Privacy for Professionals, in the Screen Aware Early Childhood Action Kit.

Ultimately, the exploitation of children's privacy through datafication and surveillance is a significant threat, one that extends beyond child,

Table 6.3. Privacy Priorities for Homes With Young Children

Voice-Assisted Speakers	When smart speakers are on, they are listening! While providing on-demand content, smart speakers often record everything from children's play, to their tantrums, to sensitive conversations between parents. It is helpful to maximize privacy settings (like allowing the device to listen only when you press a button) or to consider changing to a smart speaker without recording capacity.
Social Media and Video Posts	Privacy experts advise to "share with care." Every parent has the right to choose whether images of, or details about, their child are posted by others, including friends, family, caregivers, and teachers. Researchers have found that children often resent their parents posting pictures of them on social media without their permission. Once posted, it is not possible to control what happens to images and videos that are online.
	Helpful questions for parents to ask before sharing pictures of young children include:
	• Why am I posting it? • Is this open to the public, or only viewable by friends and family I trust? • Does this platform or app collect data related to my child? • Is there a geolocation tag (location sharing) on my photo that could allow others to know where my child is? • Is there other sensitive information displayed in this photo? • Is there a less risky way to share this?
Apps and Online Games	To help keep children safe, apps and games should have strong, easy-to-read privacy statements and be specifically designed for their developmental age. Apps and online games should not allow children to share personal information or interact with strangers and should not include pop-up ads, images, or videos that encourage or allow them to click to other content.
Artificial Intelligence (AI) and Internet-Connected Toys	Playthings that feature new technologies often appear novel and fun. Unfortunately, many of these products are not regulated for child safety or privacy, creating new avenues for profiting and collecting child data, such as tracking their location, eavesdropping on their conversations and play, and promoting brand- or character-centered relationships. Until privacy regulations are established, parents and caregivers are left with the burden of researching and monitoring the security and safety of AI and Internet-connected playthings, causing many to choose to opt out of them all together.

Adapted from Screen Aware Early Childhood Action Kit, Fact and Action Sheet #8, Digital Privacy at Home.

Table 6.4: Privacy Principles and Practices

Integrity	• Selling of personal student data and/or use for commercial or marketing purposes is prohibited. • Advertising is not allowed on instructional software, apps, or websites used by children.
Security	• Encryption is used for sensitive child, family, and employee data. • Security training and support are regularly provided for all individuals with access to personal information.
Consent	• Clear policies, practices, and permissions are in place for the use and management of photos and videos of children and families. • Parental consent is required for disclosure of personal data, especially for highly sensitive information such as a child's disabilities, health, and/or disciplinary information.
Transparency	• Parents are notified of any disclosure of personal student or family information to any persons, companies, or organizations outside of the program and have clear avenues for opting out. • Any disclosure of child or family data to a third party includes clear privacy policies that state the data to be disclosed, the purpose of the disclosure, and a date for when the data will be destroyed.
Accountability	• Privacy practices uphold program, state, and national laws and policies, including those required by the Family Educational Rights and Privacy Act (FERPA), Children's Online Privacy Protection Act (COPPA), and Individuals with Disabilities Education Act (IDEA).

Adapted from Fact and Action Sheet #9, Classroom Privacy for Families, in the Screen Aware Early Childhood Action Kit.

family, and classroom levels. A world governed by algorithms and automation challenges the development of human agency across the life span, compromising the integrity of human relations, society, and culture. As scholars Andra Siibak and Giovanna Mascheroni (2021) argue, the impact of these practices is profound, and the burden of protecting children's privacy should not fall solely on parents, children, or educators. Instead, it is crucial for platforms and Internet companies to adopt business models that prioritize the well-being and rights of children, avoiding the collection of data from and about young children altogether. This shift is necessary to ensure that children can grow up in physical and virtual ecosystems that respect their rights, dignity, autonomy, and potential.

The Right to Child-Centered Design

In contrast to problematic digital design, child-centered design puts children's rights before profits and focuses on children's development and well-being.

Emerging tech design initiatives are learning how to put children's rights before profits, prioritizing child development in design. According to Katie Davis (2023), co-director of the University of Washington Digital Youth Lab, features of a child-centered approach to design include

- self-paced, flexible interactions;
- shared experiences;
- view of children as unique, with a range of cognitive and physical abilities;
- understanding of developmental vulnerabilities and avoidance of design features that exploit them;
- restrictions on dark design patterns and design abuses;
- prioritization of high-quality, enriching content;
- provision of safe and private spaces; and
- restrictions on data collection.

One such initiative, UNICEF's Responsible Innovation in Technology for Children (RITC), in partnership with university researchers, aims to design online games that contribute to children's well-being, avoid risk, and prioritize the developmental needs of children. Their research finds that paramount features in child-centered design allow children to experience control and agency; have freedom of choice; experience mastery and achievement; experience and regulate a range of emotions; feel connected to others and manage those social connections; imagine different possibilities; act on original ideas; make things; and explore, construct, and express facets of themselves and others (UNICEF, 2024).

The U.K. Age Appropriate Design Code, one of the first legislative actions to regulate the tech industry's engagement with children, institutes specific protections against detrimental use of data, geolocation, profiling, and manipulative techniques. While safety-by-design approaches are coming to the forefront of children's tech leadership, no oversight bodies have yet been established to ensure consideration of age and children's rights to privacy and agency (OECD, 2024). No matter how much or how well tech designers consider child development, tech use will always need to be balanced and real-life experiences prioritized, especially for young children.

SUMMARY OF KEY POINTS

- Cognitively, young children cannot distinguish persuasive advertisements from the program, app, or game they are watching or playing.
- Brands use techniques like advergames, kidfluencers, and age compression to get children to nag their parents to buy products.

- Persuasive design exploits children's developmental vulnerabilities through parasocial relationships and specific psychological, physical, and social manipulations.
- Children's rights to privacy and protection apply in virtual realms.
- Data collection, whether from home or school apps, can lock children into narrow data profiles that can perpetuate stereotypes and biases.
- Child-centered design, a developing field, prioritizes children's development and well-being over collecting data for profit.

APPLYING SCREEN AWARENESS

Alicia is an early childhood speech–language therapist who visits children in their homes. When she arrives at the home of her 4-year-old client, Nic, she sees that his mother is busy in the kitchen and Nic is playing a game on his mother's phone. Not wanting to abruptly remove the device, she says hello to Nic and asks what he is doing.

"Just this," Nic says, furiously tapping away but not really knowing what to do next. Alicia shows interest and sits next to Nic. She then notices a pop-up ad for diet pills with the image of a thin girl in a bikini. She gently holds onto the device with Nic and says, "Nic, this is not part of the game you're playing, it's an ad trying to sell something to us. What if, after our session, I help you find a game that doesn't have ads or interruptions. Better yet, we could think of something else fun to do, like make a foil ball for the cat to chase."

While Nic still doesn't understand the idea that an ad is what interrupts the game, he listens because Alicia is warm and sensitive. He agrees because he would like to have more fun with her after their lesson.

1. If you were Alicia, what concerns would you have about the pop-up ad?
2. How could Alicia discuss the pop-up ad with Nic's mother without making her feel guilty about letting him play on her phone?
3. How could Alicia begin to teach Nic that some online content is put there to trick us into buying things?

CHAPTER 7

Activating Screen Awareness

Communicating anything to families—nutrition information, development concerns, social scenarios, and more—is seldom simple. Communicating with colleagues can also present challenges due to preconceptions, differing values, capacity, and stress. In this chapter, you will find techniques for approaching both families and colleagues with empathy, curiosity, and information critical to children's development in a screen-immersed world. You will be encouraged to reflect on your own screen use and how those habits do or do not translate into professional settings. Finally, you'll learn about specific professional development options that support the implementation of screen awareness in early childhood settings.

EFFECTIVE COMMUNICATION STRATEGIES

As a screen-aware practitioner, getting families and colleagues on board will provide consistent, predictable messages across children's home and classroom environments. Culturally responsive, nonjudgmental communications on all levels can produce shared understandings and practical approaches to supporting children's screen encounters. Cultural responsiveness involves considering and affirming others' perspectives, respecting their values, and understanding that individuals' perspectives are influenced by their unique experiences and backgrounds. Cultural responsiveness underlies each of the screen-time communication strategies we recommend.

Appreciative Inquiry

An appreciative inquiry approach to screen-time communication with parents and caregivers is about appreciating each family's experience, strengths, and values around screens as well as constructively inquiring about how they might incorporate new knowledge to support their developing children. Appreciative inquiry, like the strengths-based foundation of the Screen-Aware Framework for Early Childhood (SAFEC), aims to first focus on what is working and then help grow that area. It also considers what activities families value most.

Building on the family's healthy screen habits and practices and introducing values-driven dialogue can be more effective than prescribing standard solutions. For example, many families value sleep, yet may not have realized that allowing a tablet as part of the bedtime routine can introduce stimulation (e.g., blue light) at a time when children need to settle down and release their day for rest. If families already charge phones in one place at night, you might suggest that they add the children's tablets to that charging station and use a book instead as part of the bedtime routine.

It's important to recognize that marketers also work hard to convince parents that screens are an educational and necessary part of childhood. Many families think they are doing the right thing by bringing a device to a restaurant or in the car. It is helpful to start from a place of appreciation that parenting is hard, no matter the circumstances. Families may depend on screens to reduce their own stress and initially "quiet" or "calm" their children. And many families have tried different ways to reduce or minimize the harmful impacts. Early childhood practitioners can ask the following questions to begin a trusting, respectful dialogue on children's screen use.

- Have you tried to establish any screen guidelines at home? What's going well?
- What approaches, tools, or practices have you tried that are helping your family flourish?
- Which practices can you build on to turn into habits? Picking one to start might help.
- How can I help support your home habits here in the classroom?
- One idea that works in the classroom is [add a healthy screen habit here]. I wonder if that is something you might like to try at home?

Seeking to learn more about the cultural and familial significance of rituals like mealtimes, academic achievement, and/or religious traditions can also help inform the appreciative dialogue.

It is also important to share information about any screen use in the classroom and any homework expectations that involve screen use. Often, parents aren't aware of the extent of screen time during an early elementary school day. Knowing that information will assist them in making decisions about screen time at home. You can also encourage them to express any concerns and questions they have about classroom screen use.

Emotion Coaching

Based on research by psychologist John Gottman (1997), emotion coaching can help parents and practitioners to use moments of intense feelings and inappropriate behavior connected to screen use to guide children to calmer, more rational reactions. Dillon Browne, the researcher who coined the term "technovoidance" described in Chapter 5, names emotion coaching as a way to help children learn healthy coping strategies (Browne, 2018) rather than turn to a screen for comfort or distraction. Expressing empathy when a child feels angry, hurt, or confused activates neurological changes that in turn allow the child to relax.

Elements of emotion coaching include recognizing the strong feelings, listening and helping the child identify the feelings, validating the feelings, and then setting limits and problem-solving. Consistent, repetitive emotion coaching can help avoid the power struggles so often identified with screen-time rules. Teaching parents to use emotion coaching when establishing screen-time rules can make what seems like an overwhelming task an opportunity for intimacy and teaching. Parents can also use the method to monitor their own strong feelings about screen use (Emotion Coaching UK, n.d.).

An example scenario might develop like this:

Parent: It seems to me you're angry when I take away your tablet.

Child: (often responds with silence or a grunt, but thinking about what you said)

Parent: Anger can be a really big feeling and it's okay. We're all angry sometimes. What's not okay is throwing your tablet or kicking the furniture. I have some ideas—we could go outside and run around, we could pound some pillows, or we could stop and think of another thing you might like to do. I know you like your Lego blocks. Is that a good idea?

Child: Maybe. Or we could walk the dog.

In this scenario, the parent first recognizes and names the hard feeling for the child. Often just putting a name to it can bring calm to the situation. Second, the parent affirms the feeling and tells the child it's normal and okay to feel that way. Finally, the parent makes some suggestions about how to work out the hard feelings and allows the child to participate in choosing a healthy option.

Family Engagement

Decades of research on engaging family systems in children's education and health care suggests that prioritizing family engagement could lead to successful implementation of screen-aware practices. Successful family engagement includes inviting families to participate in decision-making around screen use, maintaining two-way communication, engaging families in ways that are reciprocal, and providing learning activities for home and community (National Association for the Education of Young Children, n.d.). This engagement could include forming a parent–teacher committee to determine screen-use policies, sharing articles and recommendations about healthy screen habits and screen-time management in family newsletters and other communications, holding a round table where parents share tips and successes with other parents and staff, and holding workshops with local experts on the topic. The following strategies serve to support such initiatives.

Listening First. Using simple, brief surveys can help kick off screen policy implementation, make parents feel heard, avoid assumptions, and reveal cultural attitudes and family values toward screen use. Survey formats can include multiple-choice, rating scales, and open-ended questions, and surveys can be disseminated online or via paper, or conducted in-person according to family preferences. (Not all families have Internet access.) Some questions to consider:

- Does your family set screen-time limits at home?
- What do you see as the benefits of screen-time limits?
- What are your most important family traditions that include screen use? What are your most important family traditions that don't include screen use?
- Do you feel you are well-informed about how screens impact your child in and out of the classroom?
- Would you be interested in serving on our new Screen-Aware Committee of parents and educators to help develop screen-aware policies for our program?
- Would you like to share any other suggestions or needs related to screen use at home or in the classroom?

Family feedback can help you determine how best to implement screen-aware practices for your unique community. Offering a free printed version of the Screen Aware Early Childhood Action Kit may serve as an incentive to complete the survey.

Foster Shared Understanding. The Screen Aware Early Childhood Action Kit can provide the information, framing, policies, and practices to meet the needs of families and practitioners. The fact and action sheets can serve as topics for newsletter articles, conversation starters for parent meetings, and specific guides for implementing the Screen-Aware Framework for Early Childhood (SAFEC) in your setting. Once parents, practitioners, and administrators share understandings about screen awareness, it is easier to prepare shared goals for children's success. Sharing these and other responsive resources—such as the Be Tech Wise series by the American Speech-Language-Hearing Association and the Screen Time Action Network (https://identifythesigns.org/resources-for-families/), the Screen Sense tools from Zero to Three (https://www.zerotothree.org/screensense/), and

edtech information from Everyschool (https://www.everyschool.org/the
-edtech-triangle)—makes it easier for families to feel connected.

Keep It Strengths-Based. Starting from an assumption that all families
have potential and power regarding screen awareness creates a hopeful
rather than discouraging tone. Hearing families' struggles with screen use
and how they have learned to navigate screen issues will help you transition
the conversation to screen-aware principles. Encouraging people to look for
their successes will help them feel proud and hopeful that they can tackle
screen management as they have handled other parenting challenges. It will
promote authenticity and honesty in conversations that might otherwise
revert to guilt and hiding or "cheating" on ideas that have been exchanged.

Keep It Playful and Positive. As established in Part I, play is foundational to child development. Using play and playful activities to teach children
and educate parents and colleagues about screen awareness can create a
cooperative, collaborative environment, which helps avoid strong or defen-
sive reactions. Joining children in their play and weaving in the principles
of screen awareness will help them develop a sense very early that devices
are only *part* of life, not central to their existence. Positive stories that incorporate cultural and community values can make screen awareness just
another piece of the puzzle rather than a separate, scary undertaking.

Consider Familial and Cultural Perspectives. Using translated resources
as much as possible and having translators at workshops about screen
awareness can put families at ease and encourage their participation and
commitment. You will also want to ensure that screen media you use in
the classroom represent children of many ethnicities and identities, to
create a foundation of respectful digital literacy. The Kids Inclusive and
Diverse Media Action Project (KIDMAP) at the Joan Ganz Cooney Center
has created a Diverse and Inclusive Growth (DIG) checklist (https://www
.joinkidmap.org/digchecklist) to help practitioners evaluate if digital content reflects diverse experiences, develops empathy, and uses authentic
backgrounds and traditions. The checklist supports educators with a list
of questions to ask about content, purpose, and functionality of children's
media, to determine whether it is inclusive and high-quality.

Even as practitioners help children and families navigate the screenscape, they also will continue their own professional development and often
make the case for screen awareness to colleagues, community leaders, and
policymakers. Your experiences in classrooms and homes make you well-
qualified to advocate for screen-aware practices.

PROFESSIONAL LEARNING AND DEVELOPMENT

During the early months of the COVID-19 pandemic, practitioners faced the
tremendous challenge of figuring out how to continue their work remotely.

Working with young children is usually done in close proximity and often involves physical contact, so it was especially difficult to find ways to build and maintain trust and relationships while wearing a mask, maintaining a 6-foot distance, and/or connecting via a screen. Early childhood practitioners responded with amazing resourcefulness and creativity. They drew on their knowledge of children's development and learning, tried out a range of strategies and approaches, learned from mistakes, shared ideas with families and colleagues, and gained insights from each other's experiences. They also searched the Internet for information about effective communication and teaching online, learning about how to use new platforms, apps, and programs.

Although the immediate urgency of the pandemic is over, screen-based technologies remain prominent in early learning settings. Early childhood practitioners must continue to learn about digital devices and media, as well as screen awareness, so that they can make informed decisions in the best interests of children's well-being.

The following sections focus on engagement through professional development and learning. We start with the benefits of reflecting on digital media use and habits in the personal and professional spheres. We share useful suggestions and practices for managing screen-based technologies and promoting screen-aware environments in settings that serve young children and families. Consistent with the guiding principles of the Screen-Aware Framework for Early Childhood (SAFEC), these practices are development-centered, research-informed, relationship-based, and protection-oriented.

Personal Screen Media Use

Thoughtfully reflecting on your own digital media use, as well as how you employ and model screen-based devices and media in your work with young children, is an important step toward clarifying your priorities and goals as a screen-aware practitioner.

One way to reflect on your digital media use and understand whether/what changes to make is by conducting a self-inventory, such as the Digital Flourishing Survey, offered as a free resource by the Digital Wellness Institute (see https://www.digitalwellnessinstitute.com/landing-pages/digital -flourishing-survey). The Digital Flourishing Survey, which takes about 10 minutes to complete, addresses eight dimensions of digital wellness: Communication, Relationships, Productivity, Environment, Mental Health, Physical Health, Tech-Enabled Health, and Digital Citizenship. The goal of the survey is to identify habits that are contributing to or detracting from digital wellness so that individuals can make changes that will promote their overall well-being. The Institute offers a free online microcourse about digital wellness, as well as additional resources to support and maintain digital well-being.

You may also want to consider a digital detox as a way of arriving at insights about your use of and degree of dependence on digital devices. A digital detox is simply a planned reduction or elimination of the amount of time spent online on digital devices. Usually, detox participants have a specific screen habit in mind that they want to focus on and change (Cleveland Clinic, n.d.). The detox can take a variety of forms—such as shutting off digital devices after 9:00 p.m. every night for a week, instituting a weekly "digital sabbath" day of disconnecting from all digital devices, or eliminating all digital device use except for those hours required for work.

A well-known example of a digital detox is Screen-Free Week, an annual event in which many families, child care programs, and schools participate (see https://screenfree.org/). Digital detoxes, whether one-time or ongoing, whether a day, a few days, or a week, help participants gain understandings about their habits and identify actions they want to take to enhance their digital wellness.

Resources are also available for those who are not able or ready to undertake a digital detox but still want to gain more control over their digital media use. The Center for Humane Technology provides many useful recommendations for managing personal technology use, ranging from simple to more complex (see https://www.humanetech.com/). The recommendations focus on exercising intentional control over one's own media use to promote general health and well-being and reduce sources of distraction and stress.

Insight into personal use of and dependence on digital devices is particularly important for early childhood practitioners, who serve as key screen-use role models for young children. Self-awareness helps practitioners to be more intentional in their digital device use and enhances their commitment to being an effective role model for using screens wisely.

Professional Screen Media Use

You can also gain valuable insights by reflecting on how you use screen media in your work with young children and families. Just as many of us develop habits with our personal use of screen media, we also tend to use screens in our work in certain habitual ways. Continuing to follow well-worn habits without pausing for self-examination can prevent individuals from recognizing areas for learning and professional growth—or from being open to more effective or innovative ways of using screen-based technologies.

We urge early childhood practitioners to remember that just because technology exists doesn't mean it has to be used. We strongly recommend that early childhood practitioners reflect on the essential questions related to screen awareness listed in Figure 7.1 when considering whether to use screens in classroom routines or activities. These questions can also promote thoughtful conversations among colleagues as they make decisions about screen use. It is important to reflect on the screen-aware protective factors

Figure 7.1. Essential Questions for Screen-Aware Early Childhood Practitioners

- Is a screen required for this activity?
- Which is more active, the technology or the child?
- Does screen use achieve an outcome that would not be possible without it?
- How could this task or activity be done with 3D objects or materials?
- Could this make children more dependent on screens?
- How might using a screen for this activity impact children's development and/ or behavior?

---

described in Chapter 4—responsive relationships, offline play and physical activity, time outdoors and in nature, and critical media literacy—and consider whether these factors are well integrated into routines, curriculum, and communications with families.

In addition to the Essential Questions, the Applying the Screen-Aware Framework for Early Childhood (SAFEC) tool introduced in Chapter 4 (see Figure 4.1) provokes thoughtful consideration of the SAFEC principles before making decisions about screen use.

Practitioners will also want to keep cumulative screen time in mind. Many children are exposed to or use screens for more than the amount of time per day recommended by the American Academy of Pediatrics. Any use of screens in early learning programs contributes to that total, which is another reason for practitioners to reflect on whether the benefits of employing screen-based devices or media outweigh the drawbacks of adding to children's cumulative screen time.

The Center on Media and Human Development at Northwestern University has conducted several national surveys of early childhood professionals, most recently in 2018, to learn more about their use of technology in the classroom (Pila et al., 2019). Their surveys consistently found that teachers of young children most frequently used digital cameras, with tablets becoming more common over time. Most teachers reported using cameras, tablets, and computers primarily to document children's learning and development and to show videos for children, as well as to strengthen home–school connections through communications with families. Early elementary teachers were more likely to frequently use computers, the Internet, and smartphones in their classrooms than those who worked with younger children.

About half of teachers reported that they had received professional development related to technology, particularly regarding using technology to communicate with families. Far fewer reported having received professional development in finding and navigating digital media resources and content (Pila et al., 2019). The researchers concluded that "Given the lower frequency of use for more innovative classroom practices, such findings suggest early childhood educators may not have appropriate training and support to effectively use the technology with young children" (Pila et al., 2019, p. 19).

Two meta-analyses of research studies of technology use in early childhood classrooms serving children from preschool through first grade also emphasize the need for more professional development for early childhood educators. Both concluded that one of the most influential factors in integrating technology effectively into instruction is the educator's knowledge and familiarity with the technology (Paul et al., 2023; Undheim, 2022).

With the rapid rate of technological change and the increasing expectations that teachers will use technology to promote, assess, and document student learning, ongoing professional development is needed to ensure that educators are prepared to harness the potential of any new technologies while considering any new challenges and/or unintended harmful consequences that could result. When schools adopt digital devices or programs for assessment, documentation, or instruction of preschool and early elementary students, they typically provide training for teachers when the program is first introduced. (Keep in mind that this training is often provided by the company that makes the technology and is likely to have a pro-tech stance.) Some schools even have on-site experts or professional development staff who provide the support that educators need to implement the programs effectively. When that kind of support is not available, however, teachers who have questions or encounter difficulties often must fend for themselves.

The widespread use of technology in early learning settings and the continual advances in technology can feel overwhelming. Given all the demands on teachers, it can be difficult to even find time to reflect on and identify needs for professional development related to digital media. Talking with colleagues, especially colleagues who are using technology in innovative ways, can help to narrow down the focus. Attending workshops, in-person and virtually, can also introduce you to new ideas for using digital media to promote playful learning. Sharing the information you learn at workshops with colleagues will also benefit their professional development. Keep in mind, though, that not all training and workshops are based on screen-aware principles, and some may focus on unnecessary or irrelevant uses of technology in early learning settings.

When a group of practitioners agrees on similar needs and goals for professional development, they will be able to approach administrators with a strong case for their request. It has been our experience that many early childhood practitioners are eager for more professional development related to screen awareness. Colleagues can collaborate to promote and advocate for professional development that is consistent with screen-aware principles and SAFEC.

The Action Planning tool described below can help identify professional learning and development goals.

ACTION PLANNING FOR SCREEN-AWARE PRACTICES

Practitioners who want to increase intentional and effective screen use for their personal and professional lives will find it helpful to set measurable, achievable goals. We have developed a useful resource, Action Planning With SMART Goals, for that purpose, provided in Appendix A. The SMART acronym represents key steps in action planning:

- **S**pecific: Identify a specific goal related to screen-aware practices.
- **M**easurable: Determine how to know whether the goal has been reached.
- **A**ttainable: Designate the resources needed to achieve the goal and how you might secure those resources.
- **R**elevant: Articulate its importance and who or what it supports.
- **T**imely: Set a time frame for achieving the goal.

We have shared this Action Planning form with attendees at national presentations and with groups of educators, home visitors, family support providers, and early intervention specialists, and we have received positive feedback. In many cases, colleagues collaborated at the presentation to set screen-aware goals together and identify ways to support one another and advocate for resources to achieve their goals. Working with a colleague toward the same goal can be easier and more rewarding than working on your own. We have also heard from practitioners who achieved their goals and credited the Action Planning guidelines with helping them to succeed.

Many practitioners have reported using the Action Planning format to set goals for enhancing screen awareness in their early childhood environments and establishing screen-aware practices, as well as policies, in their workplace. In the next chapter, we will explore strategies for collaborating to develop policies and partnerships. The remainder of this chapter highlights practices for creating and maintaining screen-aware environments in settings that serve young children and their families. Making a plan to implement many or all of these practices can be a solid first step in your development as a screen-aware professional.

Classroom Environments

Screen-based devices are present in most early learning settings, such as Head Start, child care programs, preschools, and elementary schools. According to national surveys, the great majority of early care and education settings have access to the Internet. The digital devices most likely to be found—and used—in classrooms for children aged infancy through 8 are cameras, computers, and tablets. Television and smartphones are also common. Far fewer early childhood environments feature interactive whiteboards and eread-ers (Pila et al., 2019). The most important considerations for educators are managing and using the technology effectively (or choosing not to use it) to promote children's learning and development.

We recommend that educators begin by reducing unnecessary distractions or intrusions from screen-based devices.

Reduce Distractions

- Store or cover screen-based devices when they are not being used for essential or required tasks.
- Turn off distracting sounds and notifications on all devices.
- Resist the urge to use screen-based music or shows during lunch or snack times.
- Use audio-only when possible. For example, when playing audio, turn the tablet around or cover the TV so the children don't see the screen.
- Minimize the time spent taking photos of children to send to families.
- Identify screen-free spaces or zones and designate them as such. (We recommend screen-free zones at drop-off and pickup times, so that adults are not distracted by devices during these critical transitions for children.)
- Have paper and pens available for adults to use to jot down notes when in the presence of children, rather than use their phones.
- When using devices around children is necessary, narrate what you're doing on your screen and let children know that you'll be with them when your task is done. This helps children make sense of an adult's divided attention without feeling ignored.

In addition to instituting these basic tips for reducing technological distraction and preventing unnecessary use, educators can consider the more complex challenge of effective, responsible screen use to promote children's learning, development, and overall well-being. Below are our recommendations for addressing that challenge.

Make Developmentally Focused Screen Choices and Policies

- Use the Essential Questions in Figure 7.1 and the Applying SAFEC tool in Figure 4.1 to determine whether screen use would be consistent with your learning objectives and SAFEC principles.
- Prioritize hands-on experiences and in-person relationships. Consider whether screen use is promoting peer interaction and collaboration among the children or encouraging isolation.

- Apply knowledge of whole-child development and the needs of individual children to determine whether screen use is beneficial and appropriate in this situation.
- Consider the cumulative time—both within and outside the early learning environment—that children are spending on screen-based devices.
- Avoid using screens for behavioral motivation, rewards, or distractions.

Maintain Responsible Use of Classroom and Personal Screen-Based Technology

- Set clear boundaries for use of screen-based devices in the environment.
- Establish policies that respect the personal privacy rights of all stakeholders (e.g., children, families, staff).
- Select screen media, apps, and activities that are free of any commercial messaging or advertising (see Chapter 6 for recommendations about how to avoid marketing ploys).
- Limit the use of screens for outsourcing tasks and activities related to teaching and learning, such as group times, transitions, and celebrations.

Guide Children as They Learn to Understand and Navigate Screen-Based Devices and Content

- Communicate and model intention, purpose, and boundaries when using screen-based devices and media in the environment. Talk about *why* it is being used, *how* it is being used, and *when* it is being used.
- Encourage children to think critically about the creation and content of screen-based media: Who made this message? Why was it made? How was it made? Who was it made for? (See the discussion of critical media literacy strategies in Chapter 5.)
- Maintain active adult engagement when implementing screen-based activities.

Many resources are available to support ongoing professional learning and development for screen-aware early childhood practitioners. Fact and Action Sheet #7 of the Screen Aware Early Childhood Action Kit contains recommendations for classroom environments. The kit also includes reproducible signs for designating screen-free zones in classrooms. Two national organizations that provide research-based, current information and resources about children's screen media use are Children and Screens and the

American Academy of Pediatrics (see https://www.childrenandscreens.org/ and https://www.aap.org/en/patient-care/media-and-children/). Children and Screens also offers webinars on a variety of topics related to the impacts of screen use on learning and development.

Home Environments

In our work with early childhood professionals, we have often had questions from practitioners about talking with families about media use in the home. Practitioners who provide services for children and families in their homes, such as early intervention specialists, home visitors, and family support providers, report feeling concerned when the TV is on in the background during their visits or when children or families appear to be heavy screen users. They worry about the distractions created by screens and the impacts on children's development, and would like to talk with families about screen use without appearing judgmental or jeopardizing their relationship.

In the first part of this chapter, we described effective strategies for communicating with families about screen use. A 2024 national survey of parents of children ages birth to 8 conducted by Common Sense Media found that "75% to 80% express consistent concerns about screen media, including worries about excessive use, effects on mental health, and the amount of inappropriate content" (Mann et al., 2025, p. 6). Yet despite these concerns, most parents are receiving little guidance about screen media from health care professionals. In the same survey, "only 23% of parents report that a pediatrician or family physician has ever discussed their child's media use and 77% have had no pediatrician guidance on this topic" (Mann et al., 2025, p. 29). Early childhood professionals play an important role in encouraging families to discuss their concerns about screen media use and providing useful suggestions. Below, we include some suggestions for supporting parents and family members who seek to manage screens with young children, reduce screen time, and optimize children's development. Many of the recommendations below come from early childhood practitioners who have shared their ideas at our presentations.

Model and Share Ideas for Nonscreen Activities. Often parents want to engage their children in nonscreen activities and play but aren't sure how to do that. Simply providing ideas and reminders for screen-free play and games can be a big help. Many early interventionists make it a point to use the materials available in the home—pots and pans, toilet paper rolls, cardboard boxes, water, measuring cups—to engage with infants and toddlers. Their goal is to emphasize to families that many simple household objects are interesting and engaging for young children, and they don't need fancy play materials.

Share Information About the Drawbacks of Background Screen Media. Many families are not aware of the distractions created by background screen media (see Chapter 3) and its impact on children's attention, focus, and language development.

Model Joint Media Engagement Strategies, With Books and With Digital Media. Joint media engagement strategies, such as those described in Chapter 5, promote children's language development and encourage positive, reciprocal interactions. It takes a little practice and encouragement to learn how to engage children using these strategies, so your modeling will be helpful.

Encourage Families to Designate Screen-Free Times and Areas. The top recommendations from the American Academy of Pediatrics for reducing the harmful effects of media use are to keep mealtimes screen-free and keep screen-based devices out of bedtime routines and bedrooms. Many families have concerns about children's sleep and are interested to learn that screens can have a negative impact on sleep.

Discuss Alternatives to Using Screens for Rewards or Punishments. Again, it will be useful for families to know about other ways to promote desirable behavior or prevent challenging behavior. In the moment, it can be difficult to think of ways to respond; a set of suggestions for alternatives can be a useful resource. You can find information about Guidance and Challenging Behavior at the website of the National Association for the Education of Young Children (NAEYC), including articles that can be shared with families (https://www.naeyc.org/our-work/families/behavior-and-development).

Share Resources. As with the recommendations for classroom environments, the Screen Aware Action Kit includes Fact and Action Sheet #6 for Home Environments. This resource is readily reproducible to share with families who want to learn more about screen awareness in the home.

Several national organizations provide family-focused resources on their websites, including ideas for nonscreen play activities appropriate for various ages as well as information about potential concerns about screen use. Parents of infants and toddlers will find a wealth of resources at the Zero to Three website (see https://www.zerotothree.org/resources/for-families/). The American Speech-Language-Hearing Association (ASHA) offers free reproducible pamphlets about being "tech wise" with babies, toddlers, and preschoolers at its website (see https://identifythesigns.org/resources-for-families/), along with information about children's development of communication skills. The American Academy of Pediatrics offers research-based information and resources about children's media use at its parenting website at https://www.aap.org/en/patient-care/media-and-children. And Fairplay for Kids provides an extensive online or printable guide to choosing apps, online videos, and connected tools and devices for preschoolers, titled *Safe, Secure, and Smart: A Guide to Choosing Tech for Your Preschooler* (available at https://fairplayforkids.org/pf/safe-secure-smart/).

As discussed in Chapter 4, knowledge of parenting and child development is one of the key protective factors for building family strengths and empowering families to take action to promote children's well-being. The suggestions we have provided here support families in understanding the impact of screens on children's development and help them develop agency in preventing potential harms.

SUMMARY OF KEY POINTS

- Conversations with families and colleagues about screen-related issues and concerns can be challenging. Maintaining a nonjudgmental approach that encourages two-way communication about participants' values, perspectives, and goals will help to promote shared understandings about screen use.
- Effective communication strategies involve listening, recognizing, and valuing the perspectives and experiences of others, focusing on strengths, and staying positive.
- Parents and practitioners can use the technique of emotion coaching to guide children's strong feelings about screen use, as well as their own.
- Early childhood practitioners benefit from ongoing professional development to manage and use screen-based technology effectively in their own lives and in early care and education settings.
- Action planning using SMART goals is an effective tool for identifying steps toward enhancing your screen awareness.
- A range of recommended practices and resources are available to help practitioners reduce distractions from and dependence on screens and promote intentional screen use to support children's learning and development.

APPLYING SCREEN AWARENESS

Kindergarten teacher Marcus prioritizes the developmental needs of the 16 children in his class and provides many opportunities for playful, active learning. Marcus is surprised when a few of his students begin asking him for extra "star time" on the classroom tablets. He learns that when the reading specialist takes students out of the classroom in small groups for literacy support, she allows children screen time on tablets after they have completed their work successfully. Marcus believes that using screen time as an extrinsic reward distracts children from developing an intrinsic sense of satisfaction in completing their work and encourages children to think of screen use as a special treat. It also increases their time on screens during the school day. Marcus appreciates the work the reading specialist does with students to enhance their literacy skills but wonders whether the children could be using their time more effectively.

Marcus uses the Applying SAFEC checklist (Figure 4.1) to determine whether his concerns are justified. He believes that the checklist supports his uneasiness about using screen time as a reward and decides to talk with the reading specialist to gain a better understanding of her teaching strategy and to share his concerns. Marcus values the reading specialist as a colleague and does not want to jeopardize their relationship.

1. Do you agree with Marcus that his concerns are justified? What aspects of the Applying SAFEC checklist seem particularly relevant to this situation?
2. In thinking about the communication strategies described in this chapter, what approach(es) could Marcus use to engage the reading specialist in discussion about screen use? If you were Marcus, how would you approach this conversation?
3. How could Marcus use the Action Planning With SMART Goals tool to plan for his conversation with his colleague and/or to work with her on the goal of avoiding the use of screen time as a reward?

CHAPTER 8

Establishing Policies and Partnerships

Anyone who has ever worked in an early care and education program or an elementary school quickly learns that there are policies governing everything from snacks and meals to guidance and discipline. In this chapter, we explore the reasons why policies matter and identify the screen-based technology issues most likely to be addressed in program, local/state, and national policies. We discuss partnerships that inform and strengthen policy development and implementation. And we emphasize ways in which early childhood practitioners can influence and shape policy development. Learning to develop policies and partnerships will bolster your arguments and strengthen your resolve. Your relationships with the young children and families you serve and understanding of child development make you uniquely qualified to develop partnerships and advocate for policies on any level.

PROGRAM/SCHOOL-LEVEL POLICIES

Policies are rules intended to guide practitioner decision-making and inform their actions and choices. Policies established for early care and learning environments focus on keeping children (and staff) safe and healthy while also communicating the values and goals of the program or school. At the program or school level, policies serve multiple important purposes, including but not limited to the following:

- Clarifying and enacting program/school values and goals
- Guiding practitioner decision-making and practices
- Informing curricular choices (learning experiences, materials, schedule, learning environment)
- Communicating to families about program goals and the rationale behind practitioner decisions
- Ensuring that relevant regulations and requirements are met

Because screen use affects children's health, development, and learning, program and school policies governing screen-based devices and media have become increasingly common and necessary. It may be surprising, however, to learn that many early learning settings still do not have specific policies related to screen technology. Although most (58.5%) early childhood practitioners responding to a national survey indicated that their school/program has specific policies about using technology for instructional purposes, over a quarter (25.5%) reported that their setting did not have policies and another 16% were not sure if policies existed (Pila et al., 2019).

We encourage all early childhood practitioners to inquire about screen-related policies during job interviews or orientations to any new position. If a program does not have any written policies about screen use, that is a red flag. Having clear guidance about screen technology supports staff members by clarifying the program's goals and values. Staff members also benefit from being able to refer to written policies in conversations with parents about screen use in the program. If your program or school does not have screen-related policies, or if the policies are outdated, unclear, or inconsistently implemented, you will find the following sections about policy development useful in advocating for policy creation and/or revision.

Policy Development

Policies related to screen media use should act as an extension and demonstration of the program's focus on children's overall well-being and healthy development (Walker, 2022). The commitment to promote children's well-being should underlie the policymaking process. As the NAEYC/Fred Rogers Center *Position Statement on Technology and Interactive Media as Tools in Early Childhood Programs Serving Children From Birth Through Age 8* states, "Above all, the use of technology tools and interactive media should not harm children" (2012, p. 5). This ethical responsibility should take precedence in establishing screen-aware program and school policies.

Screen-use policies can be contentious, especially if they are put in place without consultation or collaboration with key stakeholders or are not based on research and expert advice. When policies are developed collaboratively, it is more likely that participants will have shared understandings about how to interpret and implement them effectively. We advise seeking input and feedback from key stakeholders—staff and families—throughout the policy development process. We recommend an iterative process, with a small group or individual charged with convening discussions, drafting policies, and then bringing drafts back to the larger group for review and discussion (Cantor & Cornish, 2016). The Action Planning With SMART Goals tool described in Chapter 7 (and included in Appendix A) can be useful during the early stages of this process.

In developing a technology use policy, it makes sense to begin by identifying goals and values. A facilitated discussion around key questions can help to kick-start this process. Here are some examples of questions that will help to focus the discussion:

- What do we know about how young children develop and learn?
- What do we believe are the essentials of a high-quality early learning environment?
- What are our concerns and questions about screen use in a high-quality early learning environment?

These discussions should elicit points of agreement as well as begin to identify aspects of screen use that need to be addressed in policy. As discussions continue, participants may find it helpful to review the NAEYC and Fred Rogers Center Position Statement (2012) as well as relevant child care licensing regulations and/or accreditation criteria. The McCormick Center for Early Childhood Leadership has created a list of guiding questions related to technology usage in early childhood programs, organized around four main topics: children's technology usage; families and media; equipment, software, and data management; and staff technology usage (McCormick Center, 2014). These topics indicate the scope that technology policies may take into consideration.

Regarding children's technology use, the McCormick Center questions focus on how technology can be/is used to support children's development and overall well-being, as well as play and exploration (see https://mccormickcenter.nl.edu/library/technology-usage-in-your-early-childhood-program-questions-to-consider/). The list also includes the important question, "What research or evidence exists demonstrating the usage of the technology as an effective teaching strategy?" The McCormick Center list provides a helpful foundation that can be built on or tailored to a particular type of early learning setting or age group. The questions, when used in combination with the guiding principles of the Screen-Aware Framework for Early Childhood, can lead to strong and clear policies.

Putting policies into writing helps to prevent misunderstandings and promote consistency. If you have ever worked in a setting where you've been told that "there's no written policy, but we usually do it this way," you'll recognize the value of having written policies to consult. It is most useful for all concerned when written policies employ clear language and avoid ambiguous terms. For example, a policy that states simply that "screen technology can only be used for educational purposes" without clarifying *how* the educational value is determined could be open to a broad range of interpretations.

Once a policy has been adopted and implemented, soliciting feedback about its clarity and effectiveness will also be important. Building in a feedback process when new policies are adopted will provide information about how policies are being received and implemented and whether they are being implemented consistently. It can also be helpful to have a transition plan for putting new policies into place, so practitioners have time to become familiar with and identify their questions about the policies before implementing them.

Given the rapid changes in screen-based devices and content, we recommend clarifying what staff should do if they encounter a device or situation not covered by existing policy. The McCormick Center (2014) suggests that "Where no policy or guidelines exist, [staff] must use their professional judgment and avoid actions or posts that adversely impact the program, fellow staff members, children, and families," while also recommending that staff talk with their immediate supervisor when such situations arise.

Program/School Partners

Optimally, policies at the program or school level should also reflect the specific concerns and priorities of the community. It is unlikely that screen-related policies will capture and represent all the different perspectives of a range of stakeholders, but attempts to learn about those perspectives are valuable in building relationships and trust. Establishing partnerships with families and community members will promote shared understandings of school and program policies across other settings that serve young children and will also encourage implementation of similar policies.

Family Partners. As we have emphasized throughout this book, families have their own questions, concerns, and challenges regarding children's screen use. Seeking input from families informs the policy development process. A few key questions to ask families include the following:

- What do you want to know about screen use in this program?
- What concerns do you have about your child's screen use, at home and in this setting?
- What challenges are you experiencing? What guidance/parameters would be helpful?
- What skills and expertise do you bring?

Families are likely to have specific concerns about children of different age groups—screen use for school-age children is very different from screen use for infants, for example. The policies your program or school develops should reflect the issues associated with various age groups, with child development as the North Star. Discussions on screen-related topics will also bring out areas where families would like additional information and resources.

Interdisciplinary Partners. Within an early care and education program or elementary school setting, there are multiple stakeholders who could potentially be involved with and/or impacted by screen-use policies. Seeking input from these stakeholders during the policy development process can help to ensure that screen-related policies are implemented consistently within the program or school. Potential partners within programs and schools include special educators, general educators, librarians, health care personnel, occupational and speech therapists, guidance counselors, social workers, and early interventionists.

It's also worthwhile to consider partnerships across closely related settings—preschool programs and kindergartens, elementary schools and after-school programs, and general education and special education services. Sharing information and resources about screen-related policies with librarians, health care providers, and family support services in the community can lead to greater support for the policies enacted in your program or school. When community programs that serve the same young children promote consistent messages about screen media use, that can create a powerful support network for families, which in turn strengthens screen-aware protective factors.

Screen-Aware Program and School Policies

An important first step for any program or school seeking to establish screen-aware policies is to review existing policies. Sometimes policies are created in response to specific situations; for example, one program we know of required all teachers to have their cellphones at hand during the day so that they could use translation apps to enhance communication with English language learners and families. While an immediate response may be necessary, creating policies in a reactive rather than holistic way can lead to a hodgepodge of policies that do not seem connected to overarching goals.

The Screen-Aware Framework for Early Childhood (SAFEC) can serve as a touchstone. Screen-aware policies in early childhood environments should promote healthy development; be informed by research; support and strengthen relationships; and be oriented toward protection. Ideally, policies related to screens are integrated into a program/school philosophy and network of policies that nurture child development and learning and promote screen-aware protective factors—responsive relationships, play and physical activity, time outdoors and in nature, and critical media literacy.

For early childhood practitioners, the most immediate concern is to understand and implement program and school policies that affect their work with children and families. Educators benefit when programs and schools have comprehensive and clearly communicated screen-aware policies related to children's screen use, data storage and use, personal use of technology by staff, and data privacy protections for children, families, and staff.

Children's Screen Use. In developing screen-aware policies, early care and education programs must also consider related screen-time regulations, such as state child care licensing rules. (Not all state licensing regulations include screen-related rules.) Regulations may specify some aspects of usage, such as New York State's rule that "television and other electronic media" must be turned off during meals and naptimes in child care centers (New York State Division of Child Care Services, 2021). Some state licensing regulations include ambiguous wording, such as stating that screen media can only be used as part of a developmentally appropriate or educational activity. Program policies will be more useful if their language is clear and detailed.

Most elementary schools today have adopted screen-based devices and media for a variety of purposes. Children in kindergarten and the primary grades typically use technology throughout the school day as part of the instructional program, and educators use technology to teach, assess, and document student learning. Schools may already have policies at the building or district level about what software or apps to use (and what not to use) and under what circumstances. Some schools may have guidelines related to the maximum amount of time children spend on screens during the day. At the same time as educational technology use has increased in schools, school administrators have also become increasingly concerned about student cellphone use during the school day. Although children ages 8 and under are less likely than preteens and teenagers to have cellphones with them in school, they will be subject to any school policies related to restricted use of phones as well as other devices like smart watches.

Data Storage and Use. The goal of any policies related to data storage and use is protection—of children, families, and early childhood practitioners. For early childhood practitioners, probably the most relevant aspect of data storage and use has to do with policies related to sharing photos and videos. Program policies should address key questions:

- Who can take photos and videos of the children?
- What device(s) can be used?
- How can photos and videos be shared?
- How are parental permissions secured and honored?

We recommend that policies require practitioners to use a digital camera provided by the school or program to take photos and videos of the children, rather than using their personal smartphone camera. Photos and videos should be shared through secure platforms, rather than on social media sites. Having parents sign permission and release forms related to photos of their children helps to acquaint them with the policies around data privacy.

There are many good reasons to take photos and videos of children in early learning settings—documenting their learning and development, sharing with families eager to know about their child's day, recording key accomplishments for the child to revisit later. But as tempting as it may be to whip out the camera to record a key moment, it's also important to consider whether the camera is creating technoference, getting in the way of responsive interactions and relationships. Constant documentation can be confusing or distracting for children. As noted in "Classroom Privacy for Professionals," Fact and Action Sheet #10 in the Screen Aware Action Kit, "Documentation can impede on the interactions and activities of young children, violate a child's sense of autonomy, or promote performative or extrinsic motivation."

Personal Use of Technology by Staff. Program/school policies related to staff technology use should focus on preventing technoference during the times when practitioners are with children or families. We recommend that practitioners limit their use of cellphones or smart watches to emergency use, both in the classroom and on the playground. Use of personal technology distracts practitioners from the children and models dependence on devices. Having clear boundaries related to personal device use protects the early childhood practitioner as well as the children. Personal use of technology can also be distracting during interactions with colleagues and families and may convey a lack of interest in the interaction, which can damage relationships.

Educators will want to consider how their personal use of social media can impact their relationships with students, families, colleagues, and employers. Teachers' social media accounts are open to public scrutiny and potential misinterpretation. Practitioners will need to protect not only their own data but also their professional image. The Educator Toolkit for Teacher and Student Privacy, a free online resource created by the Parent Coalition for Student Privacy and the Badass Teachers Association (2018), provides a detailed set of tips for educators to follow when using social media for personal purposes.

Digital Privacy Protections. Protecting the privacy of children and families is a key element of screen-aware program policies. In Chapter 6, we discussed children's digital privacy rights as well as concerns about privacy violations and recommended practices to safeguard children's privacy, at home and in the classroom. Detailed recommendations for protecting digital privacy can also be found in the Educator Toolkit mentioned above. The U.S. Department of Education provides specific information for early childhood educators at the website of the Student Privacy Policy Office (see https://studentprivacy.ed.gov/audience/early-childhood-educators). These can be valuable resources in developing policies to promote digital privacy. When such policies do not exist in their program or school, practitioners can refer to these resources to ensure that they follow recommended practices for protecting privacy.

LOCAL/STATE LEVEL

While program- and school-level policies are essential for cultivating and sustaining screen awareness, community-, municipal-, and state-level support can reinforce screen awareness for young children and their families.

Community Partners

Screen-aware policies are not only about screen use. Screen awareness also encompasses policies to build and enhance protective factors, such as promoting physical activity and play, increasing time outdoors and in nature, and sharing resources and information. Enlisting a broad base of community partners in these efforts can help strengthen protective factors for young children and their families.

Parents recognize the benefits of outdoor play and want their children to have more of it. In response to a 2017 Gallup survey about play time, more than half of parent respondents wanted more outside time for their children ages 2–10 but saw several barriers to getting their children outside more. Parents identified weather conditions, safety concerns, and lack of areas to play outside as significant barriers. Substantial percentages of parents surveyed also stated that their children preferred being inside using screen media and had very busy schedules that didn't allow for increased time outdoors (Gallup, 2017).

Many community organizations and individuals, such as health care providers and mental health professionals, are deeply committed to the goal of promoting children's overall health and development. Increasing physical activity, time outdoors and in nature, and promoting play and exploration are integral to the missions of nature centers, museums and discovery centers, play/exploration centers (such as gyms and ski areas), and parks and recreation programs. Other organizations committed to supporting young children and their families include parent/teacher associations, libraries, Boys & Girls Clubs, YMCAs, and faith-based organizations. All of these community members are likely to be willing partners in efforts to create more screen-free spaces in the community and establish more accessible outdoor play spaces and natural play areas.

Many cities, small communities, and school districts in the United States have worked with nonprofit associations to create "pop-up play stations" in public areas to encourage children's play and create community play spaces; other communities have built "adventure playgrounds" where children can engage in active, open-ended play. Early childhood practitioners can also influence the creation of more play spaces in their community by sharing their concerns with local officials, voting in local elections, and working with community zoning boards.

A collaborative endeavor such as creating a list of screen-free spaces in the community, including parks, playgrounds, natural spaces, and beaches, provides a useful resource for families and emphasizes the community's commitment to children's well-being. We have known several screen-aware partners who supported families by providing them with lists of community restaurants that do not have screens, thus helping to reduce nonconsensual media encounters and promote family connections. Screen-Free Week,

National Day of Unplugging, and Digital Wellness Week efforts also involve multiple community partners working together to promote alternatives to screen-based activities.

Screen-Aware Policies

At the local and state levels, practitioners have opportunities to influence policy development in school districts and in state regulations related to early learning programs. These are levels at which screen-use policies for early learning settings as well as the protective factors of physical activity and time outdoors are often established.

School District Technology Policies. Educational technology involves substantial costs of time, energy, and money for school districts. Yet sometimes decisions about purchasing and/or using screen-based programs and apps are made without significant input from key stakeholders, including educators. Early childhood practitioners can influence technology adoption decision-making by volunteering to serve on selection committees when opportunities arise. Once the technology has been adopted, it's important for practitioners to let administrators know about their experiences with and perceptions of the effectiveness of the tech. This feedback can help to influence how the tech is used and promote more intentional, effective use—or, in some cases, can influence the decision to stop using ineffective or unnecessary tech.

The New York Times reporter who covers tech in schools, in writing about highly publicized attempts by schools to regulate cellphone use, describes the cellphone policies as part of a larger issue: "Technology rules and safeguards in schools often lag far behind student use and abuse of digital tools" (Singer, 2024). Because technology advances faster than policy, schools are struggling to keep up. Educators often bear the brunt of what happens when policies governing tech use are poorly conceived or nonexistent. Many educators find it more productive and rewarding to advocate for or become involved in efforts to develop policies related to technology than to wait for such policies to be developed.

Digital competencies and digital citizenship are significant elements of screen-based policies (Walker, 2022). Ideally, these aspects are taught and reinforced in schools. Competencies—skills and abilities needed to effectively use technology—may be spelled out in state educational standards and district policy. Schools can teach children, overtly and by example, to be conscientious and respectful users of screen media and avoid using screen media for harm. School district policies and state educational standards also address minimum amounts of physical activity required during the school day or week as well as outdoor recess policies.

Educators can influence these policies by participating in formulation and providing feedback. When states develop or review standards, they often request volunteers to serve on committees to revise existing standards or develop new standards. Drafts of the revisions are disseminated for feedback, and the feedback from practitioners is reviewed and taken into account. These are important opportunities for sharing expertise and insights to influence policy.

Families and educators are also working together to advocate for school policies that promote screen awareness. One example is the Digital Balance Resolution adopted by the Montgomery, MD, County Council in early 2023 after a parent-led campaign. The Montgomery County Digital Balance Resolution calls for the county's public schools to:

1. Limit screen time in the classroom systematically unless it aids in education or assists students who are receiving services or accommodations.
2. Finish and release the Montgomery County Public Schools–developed digital best practices that have been under development for a while.
3. Monitor digital resources and screen time to ensure that they are age-appropriate, academically advantageous, and purposeful.
4. Train staff to monitor students for excessive screen time symptoms.
5. Provide readily available offline options that do not exclude or embarrass the child.
6. Select curricula that include up-to-date nondigital materials when possible.
7. Develop curriculum guidance that includes physical materials like books, outdoor education, and hands-on learning.
8. Minimize digital testing, as it can be stressful and lead to digital practice.
9. Immediately use hard-copy resources in elementary schools.
10. Immediately discourage digital gaming and screen time rewards or breaks.
11. Immediately ensure that nondigital books and puzzles are available for free time.

(Carassa, 2023)

Digital Balance Resolutions such as this help to reduce unnecessary and potentially harmful screen use in schools.

Child Care Licensing Regulations. State child care licensing regulations are routinely reviewed and revised every few years. As part of the revision process, state administrators solicit the input of early childhood practitioners. Often, public hearings will be held (in person and online) for public comment. These are valuable opportunities for early childhood professionals to express their concerns and recommendations related to screen time, screen use, and requirements for physical activity, play, and time outdoors. In some states, early childhood professionals will be invited to work on committees engaged in clarifying and/or revising state licensing laws.

Early childhood practitioners can also support one another in interpreting and implementing existing regulations, as well as sharing examples of and resources about screen-aware policies. In 2015, the state of Louisiana enacted new regulations prohibiting the use of electronic devices in programs serving children under age 2 and restricting screen time to a maximum of 2 hours per day for children ages 2 and older. Child care programs were required to develop written policies about electronic device use as well as policies about minimum physical activity requirements (at least 60 minutes per day). A coalition of child care professionals, academics, program directors, and community health professionals worked on developing resources to support Louisiana child care programs in understanding and implementing the new regulations (Staiano et al., 2018). This resulted in the *Louisiana Screen Time Regulations Toolkit for Early Childhood Education Centers* (Louisiana Department of Health, 2024), a free resource. The toolkit is designed to "assist child care providers in Louisiana to reduce or eliminate screen time in child care centers." It includes information about the regulations, a brief overview of the potential impact of screen time on young children, a screen time self-assessment for centers, guidelines for developing policies, sample newsletters for families, and the template for a 15-minute parent workshop (see https://www.pbrc.edu/research-and-faculty/scientific-reports/Louisiana%20Screen%20Time%20Regulations%20Toolkit%20NEW%20AAP%20Guidelines.pdf). The toolkit is an excellent example of early childhood practitioners collaborating and using their knowledge and expertise to cultivate screen awareness.

NATIONAL LEVEL

The screen-related issues most likely to be discussed and addressed at the national level through federal policy are those related to increasing access, protecting children from online harm, guarding data privacy, and monitoring the tech industry. Policies related to ensuring greater access to the Internet are developed at the federal level. Examples of such policies include increasing broadband Internet access, providing federal funding to restore Internet access after emergencies, and making digital apps more accessible to accommodate variations in language, literacy, and ability. Many federal offices, for example, must review materials and documents for accessibility and achieve accessibility standards prior to releasing them to the public.

Regulations to protect digital privacy and safety, especially of children, fall under the purview of the federal government. Notable federal laws intended to safeguard children online include:

- Children's Internet Protection Act (CIPA): requires schools and libraries to adopt and implement Internet safety policies.
- Children's Online Privacy and Protection Act (COPPA): imposes restrictions and requirements on websites to protect children's identities and personal information.
- Protecting Children in the 21st Century Act: requires the Federal Trade Commission to provide nationwide education about practices to promote children's online safety.
- Family Educational Rights and Privacy Act (FERPA): protects the sharing of personal information related to school records.
- Health Insurance Portability and Accountability Act (HIPPA): protects the sharing of personal information related to health records. (Walker, 2022, pp. 505–506)

Through the Children's Online Privacy and Protection Act (COPPA), the federal government does impose some restrictions on websites and companies to monitor the content that they share online; however, COPPA has not been updated since 1998, before tablets, smartphones, and children's apps were invented.

To a large extent, tech companies are responsible for monitoring their own content and removing or not allowing content that is harmful to mental or physical health. Debate continues as to the role of the federal government in making these companies accountable when they fail to meet their own guidelines or their guidelines are inadequate. Tech companies counter that such restrictions violate the First Amendment guaranteeing the right to free speech. Proponents of increased regulation argue that legislation intended to protect children online does not violate free speech, does not impose censorship, and does not restrict users' rights to access information; rather, it requires tech companies to "prioritize minors' well-being over user engagement or profits" (Grosshans, 2024, n.p.). These debates are likely to continue, and their outcome will affect the future direction of federal policies related to children's online safety.

Influence as a Private Citizen

Like all citizens, early childhood practitioners can influence federal policymaking through exercising their vote and contacting elected officials to express their views. As part of the process of deciding which candidates to support for elected office, practitioners can and should become familiar with the candidates' positions on screen-related issues such as data privacy protections and measures to prevent the exploitation of children online. If candidates have not expressed their views on screen-related issues, citizens can contact their campaign offices to ask about those views. Campaign staff want to know what voters care about and what concerns them. One of the most important steps practitioners can take as screen-aware citizens is to vote for candidates whose positions seem most likely to promote the well-being of young children.

Constituents can share their views with their elected officials by contacting congressional offices via phone, letter, or email. Elected officials often seek input from their constituents through town halls (in person or online). Constituents may contact their elected officials with concerns at any time, but it is especially important for early childhood practitioners to share their views about any proposed legislation affecting children's health and well-being.

Influence as a Member of a Professional Organization

Although your vote and views carry influence, you can have even greater impact on policy as part of a broader group of concerned stakeholders. Many professional associations engage in coordinated efforts to influence the development or revision of federal policies. There is strength in numbers, and belonging to a professional association amplifies your voice. Often, professional associations organize campaigns to bring issues affecting children and families to the attention of policymakers. They may provide training for members in effective messaging, as well as coordinating visits to legislators and legislative staff. For example, the National Association for the Education of Young Children (NAEYC) offers an annual Public Policy Forum that includes advocacy training and visits to House and Senate members. When relevant pieces of legislation are up for a vote, many professional associations provide guidance and reminders about contacting legislators.

Participating in policy development may not be among the top reasons why early childhood practitioners choose to go into the field. It is not surprising, though, that with their commitment to children's well-being, practitioners care deeply about efforts to improve conditions for children in the classroom, in the community, and in the wider world.

SUMMARY OF KEY POINTS

- Policies are more likely to be implemented effectively if they are clear and have been developed through a process that involves key stakeholders.

- Early childhood practitioners can influence policy development at the program/school, local/state, and national levels.

APPLYING SCREEN AWARENESS

Kai (who uses they/them pronouns) is a new preschool teacher in a child care center serving children ages 6 weeks through 5 years. Kai loves their center's emphasis on relationships and playful learning, but they are concerned that the center currently has no written policies related to screen use. Instead, teachers are told to follow the state child care licensing requirements, which state: "If television or other electronic visual media is used, it must be part of a planned developmentally appropriate program with an educational, social, physical or other learning objective that includes identified goals and objectives" (New York State Division of Child Care Services, 2021).

Kai quickly realizes that their fellow teachers interpret this rule in their own ways. Some colleagues use screens to share videos related to curricular content, one shows videos for children who don't nap, and all use their phones to take photos of the children for documentation purposes. Kai would like more guidance about technology use and wants to support their center in developing guidelines.

1. How could Kai go about working with administration and colleagues to clarify or develop guidelines?
2. What tools or resources could they use?
3. If you were Kai, what screen-related policies would be of most immediate concern to you? Why?

Epilogue
Advocating for Screen Awareness

Practitioners and parents ask us all the time, "What is the right amount of screen time for young children?" and "It's okay to use educational media, right?" We respond that it's not that simple. The screenscape has become a complex web of content and design, with thousands of apps, games, and virtual environments available and marketed to children, even though they have not been created with child well-being or core developmental needs in mind. Our overarching goal in writing this book was to help early childhood practitioners navigate the challenges of caring for and educating young children in a screen-based world.

We created the Screen-Aware Framework for Early Childhood (SAFEC) to serve as a guide for making decisions about screen use that focus on development, are informed by research, strengthen relationships, and protect children from potentially harmful effects of screens. We have provided information about young children's developmental needs and how screens can positively or negatively impact development, learning, and relationships. We have highlighted noteworthy research about potential harms posed by screen use and identified the insidious features that are often built into screen-based media and devices. We have emphasized the protective factors that will help to shield children and families from harmful effects. And we have recommended an array of screen-aware practices and policies that practitioners can implement or influence, along with useful tools and resources to aid in that work.

We hope that by this point you have begun using screen-aware practices in your own personal and professional spheres. Given what you have learned about the potential harms of screens and the benefits of intentional, screen-aware practices, you may be fired up about screen awareness and eager to do more! The skills and attributes needed to be an effective early childhood practitioner—knowledge of the field, the ability to teach and to learn, effective communication, cultural competency, empathy, and optimism—are also valuable qualities for advocates. It's no surprise that many early childhood professionals are drawn to advocacy and are compelling and persuasive champions for children and families.

Becoming an effective advocate starts with being well-informed. In the digital age, that means being informed about the research on screens and developmental impacts, screen-aware practices and policies, and the perspectives and experiences of stakeholders. It also involves learning about the decision-making processes that govern screen use in your program or school. As we've described in Chapter 8, early childhood practitioners can take advantage of opportunities to get involved in decision-making about technology and use their knowledge of child development and learning to determine if tech is relevant and appropriate.

Effective advocates persuade others that practices and policies need to change. Explaining the harms caused by those policies (or the lack of policies) isn't always enough—it's also powerful to present alternatives. Which screen-aware practices are you most eager to try? Who will you need to convince before implementing them? Sharing information about screen-aware practices and strategies can transform settings that serve young children and families, including homes and classrooms. Families and colleagues will also appreciate suggestions for screen-free activities that promote protective factors, create balance, and help young children thrive.

The time is ripe for screen-aware advocacy, as more and more families and educators are becoming concerned about the impact of screens on children from infancy through the teen years and the extensive use of screens in schools and educational settings. For example, the uptick in concerns about cellphone use in schools has led to a phone-free schools movement. Parents, educators, and school administrators are collaborating to institute cellphone bans during the school day or to promote pledges to wait until 8th grade to give children phones. These movements are often led by parents of kindergarteners and first-graders, because they want to ensure that cellphone restrictions are in place before their children reach their tweens (Krueger, 2024).

Many practitioners embrace screen awareness as an essential element of educating children in the digital age. As we noted in Chapter 8, there is strength in numbers. Not only can advocates amplify their concerns by participating in professional associations, they can also find support and inspiration from working with like-minded colleagues, in both their physical and virtual environments. The Screen Time Action Network at Fairplay— an international coalition of practitioners, educators, advocates, and parents working to reduce excessive and harmful screen use in childhood and keep children safe online—is one such group. Membership in the Network is free. The three of us met professionally at the Action Network's inaugural conference in Boston in 2018. As founding director, Jean has overseen the Action Network's growth to over 3,000 members globally, and Pat and

Mindy are founding members of its Early Childhood Work Group, which created and distributed the Screen Aware Early Childhood Action Kit.

Advocacy groups like the Action Network provide opportunities for members to connect with others who care deeply about children's screen use. Members freely share resources and ideas, including their own successful advocacy efforts and how they achieved their goals. For example, Melissa, a school psychologist in Santa Barbara, California, noticed an increase in depression and anxiety in very young children concurrent with the issue of individual iPads for children in 2nd grade and under during the COVID-19 pandemic. She gathered parents, pediatricians, and other counselors to educate parents, solicited 200 signatures, and asked the Santa Barbara Unified School District to ban iPads in the early years. She also asked the district to provide parents with training on how to avoid excessive screen time. Her effort got the iPads out and the training in. Katie, a preschool teacher in Pittsburgh, Pennsylvania, successfully advocated for a Digital Balance Resolution in her school district that included banning tablets. Katie worked with Kailan, an Action Network colleague based on the West Coast, to develop Let's Grow Brain P.O.W.E.R., a free resource for schools and community programs that is intended to encourage and inspire families of young children to engage in screen-free activities that promote brain development (see https://www.letsgrowbrainpower.com). Several Action Network members have formed a task force, led by Arianna, a speech and language pathologist (SLP) from Oregon. The goal of the task force is to learn about the perspectives of fellow SLPs on screen time in order to provide information and resources to support their work.

Screen awareness, or the knowledge and practices that uphold the developmental well-being and rights of young children within a screen-based, mediacentric society, is more relevant now than ever. Tech companies profit when consumers purchase their products, whether the products enhance learning or not. An analysis of public records related to school district spending on educational technology during the pandemic found that despite spending tens of millions of dollars in pandemic funding on edtech products, school districts "have little or no evidence the programs helped students" (Binkley, 2023). While technology was useful during the pandemic to enable schools to offer remote learning, edtech companies maintain a strong hold in school systems that hasn't shown signs of abating postpandemic. And school-provided devices are increasingly making their way into homes, with nearly 1 in 5 children ages 5 to 8 using a school-provided tablet or laptop at home (Mann et al., 2025, p. 19).

As we write this book, artificial intelligence (AI) is making its way into early learning settings, the latest example of new technology being introduced before research has established its potential benefits and harms or even how it could be used effectively to promote learning. We have designed SAFEC to respond to current screenscapes as well as emerging and future digital technologies and pressures. Keeping this book handy and practicing its principles will help you feel prepared.

Advocates for practices and policies that support and promote the developmental needs of young children are urgently needed and will continue to be needed as technology continues its rapid growth and widespread infiltration into early learning settings. We hope that this book supports and inspires you to become an advocate for screen-aware practices, policies, and partnerships in your program or school, your community, and beyond.

Action Planning With SMART Goals

SCREEN AWARE early childhood

Action Planning with S.M.A.R.T. Goals

My screen aware goal:

This goal supports (circle one): PRACTICE   POLICY   PARTNERSHIP

Make it **Specific**	The outcome of my goal is:	
Make it **Measurable**	I will know I am on the path toward my goal when:	
	I will know I have achieved the goal when:	
Make it **Attainable**	Resources (e.g., time, money, people) available for my goal are:	
	Resources (e.g., time, money, people) needed for my goal are:	
	Ideas I have for securing needed resources are:	
Make it **Relevant**	My goal is important because:	
	My goal supports:	
Make it **Timely**	A start date for my goal is:	
	An end date for my goal is:	

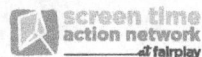

screen time action network at fairplay

Sample Phone-Free Zone Sign

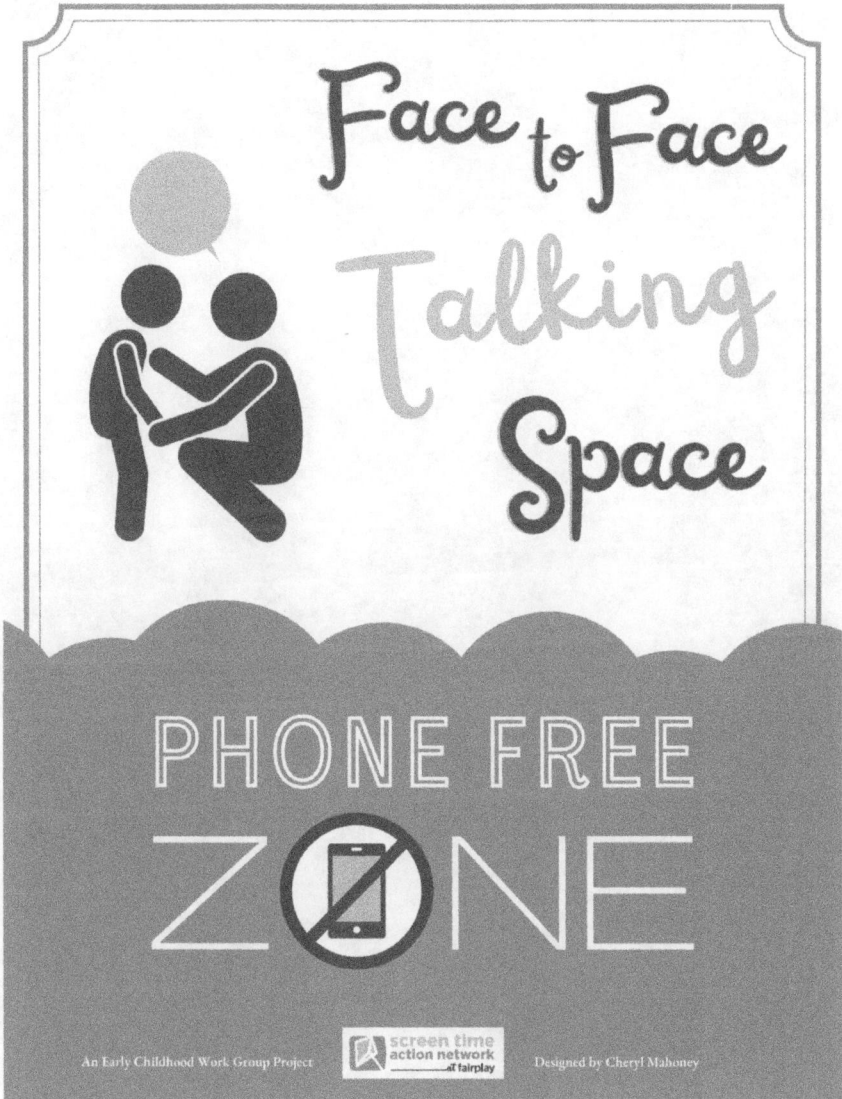

Sample Photo-Free Zone Sign

References

Abels, M., Vanden Abeele, M., Van Telgen, T., & Van Meijl, H. (2018). Nod, nod, ignore: An exploratory observational study on the relation between parental mobile media use and parental responsiveness towards young children. In E. M. Luef & M. M. Marin (Eds.), *The talking species: Perspectives on the evolutionary, neuronal, and cultural foundations of language* (pp. 195–228). Uni-Press Verlag.

Almeida, M. (2019). An immeasurable loss for psychiatry (and the world). *Journal of the National Medical Association, 111*(6), 640–641. https://doi.org/10.1016/j.jnma.2019.08.007

Altamura, L., Vargas, C., & Salmeron, L. (2023). Do new forms of reading pay off? A meta-analysis on the relationship between leisure digital reading habits and text comprehension. *Review of Educational Research, 95*(1), 53–88. https://doi.org/10.3102/00346543231216463

American Academy of Pediatrics. (2022, July 11). *Assessment of social emotional development and protective factors.* Patient Care. https://www.aap.org/en/patient-care/early-childhood/early-relational-health/assessment-of-social-emotional-development-and-protective-factors/

American Academy of Pediatrics. (2023). *Beyond spoken words: Augmentative and alternative communication (AAC).* Healthy Children. https://www.healthychildren.org/English/health-issues/conditions/developmental-disabilities/Pages/augmentative-and-alternative-communication-for-children.aspx

American Academy of Pediatrics. (2024). *Kids & screen time: How to use the 5 C's of media guidance.* Healthy Children. https://www.healthychildren.org/English/family-life/Media/Pages/kids-and-screen-time-how-to-use-the-5-cs-of-media-guidance.aspx?_gl=1*pxhyqt*_ga*NDk3Mjg1NTMwLjE3MTM1MzEzNjQ.*_ga_FD9D3XZVQQ*MTcxODExNjg3Mi4xMS4xLjE3MTgxMTY4NzIuMC4wLjA

American Academy of Pediatrics Center of Excellence on Social Media and Youth Mental Health. (n.d.). https://www.aap.org/en/patient-care/media-and-children/center-of-excellence-on-social-media-and-youth-mental-health/

American Academy of Pediatrics Council on Communications and Media. (2016a). Children and adolescents and digital media. *Pediatrics, 138*(5), e20162591. http://publications.aap.org/pediatrics/article-pdf/138/5/e20162593/1062131/peds_20162593.pdf

American Academy of Pediatrics Council on Communications and Media. (2016b). Virtual violence. *Pediatrics, 138*(1), e20151298. https://doi.org/10.1542/peds .2016–1298

Anderson, D. R., & Hanson, K. G. (2013). What researchers have learned about toddlers and television. *Zero to Three, 33(4),* 4–10.

Armstrong, A. L. (2023). Do I see me? A discussion about technology use and representation in children's media. *Young Children, 78*(5), 24–29.

Atabey, A,. & Hooper, L. (2024). International regulatory decisions concerning EdTech companies' data practices. Digital Futures for Children and 5Rights Foundation. https://eprints.lse.ac.uk/123805/1/DFC_Brief_International_regu latory_decisions_final.pdf

Auxier, B., Anderson, M., Perrin, A., & Turner, E. (2020). *Parenting children in the age of screens.* Pew Research Center. https://www.pewresearch.org/internet/2020 /07/28/parenting-children-in-the-age-of-screens/

Bank, A. M., Barr, R., Calvert, S. L., Parrott, W. G., McDonough, S. C., & Rosenblum, K. (2012). Maternal depression and family media use: A questionnaire and diary analysis. *Journal of Child and Family Studies, 21*(2), 208–216. https://doi .org//10.1007/s10826-011-9464-1

Barr, R., Kirkorian, H., Radesky, J., Coyne, S., Nichols, D., Blanchfield, O., Rusnak, S., Stockdale, L., Ribner, A., Durnez, J., Epstein, M., Heimann, M., Koch, F. S., Sundqvist, A., Birberg-Thornberg, U., Konrad, C., Slussareff, M., Bus, A., Bellagamba, F., & Fitzpatrick, C. (2020). Beyond screen time: A synergistic approach to a more comprehensive assessment of family media exposure during early childhood. *Frontiers in Psychology,* 11, 1283. https://doi.org/10.3389/fpsyg.2020.01283

Barr, R., McClure, E., & Parlakian, R. (2018). What the research says about the impact of media on children aged 0-3 years old. *Zero to Three.* https://www .zerotothree.org/resource/screen-sense-what-the-research-says-about-the -impact-of-media-on-children-aged-0-3-years-old/

Barr, R., McClure, E., & Parlakian, R. (2019). Maximizing the potential for learning from screen experiences in early childhood. *Zero to Three, 40*(2), 29–36.

Bessant, C., Ong, L., Cook, L., Hoy, M., Pereira, B., Fox, A., Nottingham, E., Steinberg, S., & Gan, P. (2023). *Exploring parents' knowledge of dark design and its impact on children's digital well-being.* Paper presented at AoIR2023: The 24th Annual Conference of the Association of Internet Researchers.

Biermeier, M. A. (2015). Inspired by Reggio Emilia: Emergent curriculum in relationship-driven learning environments. *Young Children, 70*(5), 72–79. https:// www.naeyc.org/resources/pubs/yc/nov2015/emergent-curriculum

Binkley, C. (2023, October 9). *Schools' pandemic spending boosted tech companies. Did it help US students?* Associated Press. https://apnews.com/article/edtech-school -software-app-spending-pandemic-e2c803a30c5b6d34620956c228de7987 ?utm_source=Email&utm_medium=share

Blum-Ross, A., & Livingstone, S. (2016). Families and screen time: Current advice and emerging research. *Media Policy Brief 17.* Media Policy Project, London School of Economics and Political Science. http://eprints.lse.ac.uk/66927/

Blum-Ross, A., & Livingstone, S. (2017). "Sharenting," parent blogging, and the boundaries of the digital self. *Popular Communication, 15*(2), 110–125. https://doi.org/10.1080/15405702.2016.1223300

Borges, A. (2024, March 11). A multitasker's guide to regaining focus. *The New York Times.* https://www.nytimes.com/2024/03/11/well/mind/multitasking-tips.html

Bowlby, J. (1969). *Attachment and loss* (2nd ed., Vol. I). Basic Books.

Bravender, T., & Bravender, L. S. (2020, March 13). *Nature play: A prescription for healthier children.* Contemporary Pediatrics. https://www.contemporarypediatrics.com/view/nature-play-prescription-healthier-children

Brito, R., Dias, P., & Oliveira, G. (2018). Young children, digital media and smart toys: How perceptions shape adoption and domestication. *British Journal of Educational Technology, 49*(5), 807–820. https://doi.org/10.1111/bjet.12655

Bronfenbrenner, U. (1974). Developmental research, public policy, and the ecology of childhood. *Child Development, 45*(1), 1–5. https://doi.org/10.2307/1127743

Bronfenbrenner, U., & Morris, P. A. (2006). The bioecological model of human development. In R. M. Lerner & W. Damon (Eds.), *Handbook of child psychology; Vol. 1: Theoretical models of human development* (6th ed., pp. 783–828). John Wiley & Sons.

Brown, T. T., & Jernigan, T. L. (2012). Brain development during the preschool years. *Neuropsychology Review, 22*, 313–333. https://doi.org/10.1007/s11065-012-9214-1

Browne, C. H. (2014). *The Strengthening Families Approach and protective factors framework: Branching out and reaching deeper.* Center for the Study of Social Policy. https://cssp.org/wp-content/uploads/2018/11/Branching-Out-and-Reaching-Deeper.pdf

Browne, D. (2018, December 2). Technovoidance: Managing difficult feelings with devices. *Psychology Today,* n.p. https://www.psychologytoday.com/intl/blog/why-family-matters/201812/technovoidance-managing-difficult-feelings-with-devices

Bustamante, J. C., Fernandez-Castilla, B., & Alcaraz-Iborra, M. (2023). Relation between executive functions and screen time exposure in under 6 year-olds: A meta-analysis. *Computers in Human Behavior, 145*, 107739. https://doi.org/10.1016/j.chb.2023.107739

Caine, R. N., Caine, G., McClintic, C., & Klimek, K. J. (2016). *12 brain/mind learning principles in action: Teach for the development of higher-order thinking and executive function* (3rd ed.). Corwin Press.

Cantor, P. A., & Cornish, M. M. (2016). *Techwise infant and toddler teachers: Making sense of screen media for children under 3.* Information Age Publishing.

Canvello, A., & Crocker, J. (2010). Creating good relationships: Responsiveness, relationship quality, and interpersonal goals. *Journal of Personality and Social Psychology, 99*(1), 78–106. https://doi.org/10.1037/a0018186

Carassa, T. (2023, February 10). First parent-led digital balance resolution in the U.S. passed in Montgomery County. *Montgomery County Sentinel.* https://www.thesentinel.com/communities/first-parent-led-digital-balance-resolution-in

-the-u-s-passed-in-montgomery-county/article_6a1ba696-a9a4-11ed-b5ae
-bf5c1ff75c5f.html

Carlson, F. M. (2011). *Big body play*. National Association for the Education of Young Children.

Center for the Study of Social Policy. (n.d.). *About Strengthening Families and the Protective Factors Framework*. Center for the Study of Social Policy. https://cssp.org /resource/about-strengthening-families-and-the-protective-factors-framework/

Center on the Developing Child. (2011). *In brief: Executive function: Skills for life and learning*. https://developingchild.harvard.edu/resources/inbrief-executive-fun ction-skills-for-life-and-learning

Center on the Developing Child. (n.d.). *A guide to serve and return: How your interaction with children can build brains*. https://developingchild.harvard.edu/guide/a -guide-to-serve-and-return-how-your-interaction-with-children-can-build -brains/

Centers for Disease Control and Prevention, National Center for Injury Prevention and Control, Division of Violence Prevention. (2024, May 16). *Adverse Childhood Experiences (ACEs)*. https://www.cdc.gov/aces/about/index.html

Chen, C., Chen, S., Wen, P., & Snow, C. E. (2020). Are screen devices soothing children or soothing parents? Investigating the relationships among children's exposure to different types of screen media, parental efficacy and home literacy practices. *Computers in Human Behavior, 112,* 106462. https://doi.org/10.1016/j .chb.2020.106462

Children & Screens. (2024). *Infant cognitive development and screens*. Research at a Glance. Children and Screens Institute of Digital Media and Child Development. https://www.childrenandscreens.org/wp-content/uploads/2024/08/Infant-Co gnitive-Development-At-a-Glance-Final-WEB.pdf

Christakis, D. A., Gilkerson, J., Richards, J. A., Frederick, M., Zimmerman, J., Garrison, M. M., Xu, D., Gray, S., & Yapanel, U. (2009). Audible television and decreased adult words, infant vocalizations, and conversational turns: A population-based study. *Archives of Pediatrics & Adolescent Medicine, 163*(6), 554–558.

Cleveland Clinic. (n.d.). *How to do a digital detox for less stress, more focus*. Health Essentials. https://health.clevelandclinic.org/digital-detox

Cost, K. T., Unternaehrer, E., Tsujimoto, K., Vanderloo, L. L., Birken, C. S., Maguire, J. L., Szatmari, P., & Charach, A. (2023). Patterns of parent screen use, child screen time, and child socio-emotional problems at 5 years. *Journal of Neuroendocrinology, 35*(7), e13246. https://doi.org/10.1111/jne.13246

Coyne, S. M., Rogers, A., Holmgren, H. G., Booth, M. A., Van Alfen, M., Harris, H., Barr, R., Padilla-Walker, L., Sheppard, J. A., Shawcroft, J., & Ober, M. (2023). Masters of media: A longitudinal study of parental media efficacy, media monitoring, and child problematic media use across early childhood in the United States. *Journal of Children and Media, 17*(3), 318–335. https://doi.org/10.1080 /17482798.2023.2200958

Critical Media Project. (n.d.). *Media literacies.* https://criticalmediaproject.org/media-literacies/

Danet, M., Miller, A. L., Weeks, H. M., Kaciroti, N., & Radesky, J. S. (2022). Children aged 3–4 years were more likely to be given mobile devices for calming purposes if they had weaker overall executive functioning. *Acta Paediatrica, 111*(7), 1383–1389. https://doi.org/10.1111/apa.16314

Dankiw, K. A., Tsiros, M. D., Baldock, K. L., & Kumar, S. (2020). The impacts of unstructured nature play on health in early childhood development: A systematic review. *PLoS ONE, 15*(2): e0229006. https://doi.org/10.1371/journal.pone.0229006

Dardanou, M., Unstad, T., Brito, R., Dias, P., Fotakopoulou, O., Sakata, Y., & O'Connor, J. (2020). Use of touchscreen technology by 0–3-year-old children: Parents' practices and perspectives in Norway, Portugal and Japan. *Journal of Early Childhood Literacy, 20*(3), 551–573. https://doi.org/10.1177/1468798420938445

Davis, K. (2023). *Technology's child: Digital media's role in the ages and stages of growing up.* MIT Press.

Domoff, S. E., Harrison, K., Gearhardt, A. N., Gentile, D. A., Lumeng, J. C., & Miller, A. L. (2019). Development and validation of the problematic media use measure: A parent report measure of screen media "addiction" in children. *Psychology of Popular Media Culture, 8*(1), 2–11. https://doi.org/10.1037/ppm0000163

Edwards, S., & Bird, J. (2017). Observing and assessing young children's digital play in the early years: Using the Digital Play Framework. *Journal of Early Childhood Research, 15*(2), 158–173. https://doi.org/10.1177/1476718X15579746

Elias, N., Lemish, D., Dalyot, S., & Floegel, D. (2021). "Where are you?" An observational exploration of parental technoference in public places in the US and Israel. *Journal of Children and Media, 15*(3), 376–388.

Emotion Coaching UK. (n.d.). *Elements of emotion coaching.* https://www.emotioncoachinguk.com/what-is-emotion-coaching

Erikson Institute. (2016). *Technology and young children in the digital age: A report from the Erikson Institute.* https://www.erikson.edu/wp-content/uploads/2018/07/Erikson-Institute-Technology-and-Young-Children-Survey.pdf

Escueta, M., Nickow, A. J., Oreopoulos, P., & Quan, V. (2020). Upgrading education with technology: Insights from experimental research. *Journal of Economic Literature, 58*(4), 897–996. https://doi.org/10.1257/jel.20191507

Everyschool. (2022). *The EdTech report: Research to know right now about technology in the classroom.* https://static1.squarespace.com/static/5e7f60459beb49266ae92b37/t/635000b6c9ffb178dde56ed4/1666187446585/The+EdTech+Report.pdf

Fairplay. (2015). *Advocates say "hell no Barbie" to stop Mattel from spying on kids.* https://fairplayforkids.org/advocates-say-hell-no-barbie-to-stop-mattel-from-spying-on-kids/

Fandakova, Y., & Hartley, C. A. (2020). Mechanisms of learning and plasticity in childhood and adolescence. *Developmental Cognitive Neuroscience, 42,* 100764. https://doi.org/10.1016/j.dcn.2020.100764

Federal Trade Commission. (2014, August 22). *Defendants settle FTC charges related to "Your Baby Can Read" program.* https://www.ftc.gov/news-events/news/press-releases/2014/08/defendants-settle-ftc-charges-related-your-baby-can-read-program

Felix, E., Silva, V., Caetano, M., Ribeiro, M. V. V., Fidalgo, T. M., Rosa Neto, F., Sanchez, Z. M., Surkan, P. J., Martins, S. S., & Caetano, S. C. (2020). Excessive screen media use in preschoolers is associated with poor motor skills. *Cyberpsychology, Behavior and Social Networking, 23*(6), 418–425. https://doi.org/10.1089/cyber.2019.0238

Findley, E., LaBrenz, C. A., Childress, S., Vasquez-Schut, G., & Bowman, K. (2021). 'I'm not perfect': Navigating screen time among parents of young children during COVID-19. *Child: Care, Health, & Development, 48*(6), 1094–1102. https://doi.org/10.1111/cch.13038

Flint, T. K., & Adams, M. S. (2023). Of ladles and laptops: Exploring preschool children's digital play. *Early Childhood Education Journal, 52,* 1001–1010. https://doi.org/10.1007/s10643-023-01485-9

Foreman, J., Salim, A. T., Praveen, A., Fonseka, D., Ting, D. S. W., Guang He, M., Bourne, R. R. A., Crowston, J., Wong, T. Y., & Dirani, M. (2021). Association between digital smart device use and myopia: A systematic review and meta-analysis. *The Lancet Digital Health, 3*(12), e806–e818. https://pubmed.ncbi.nlm.nih.gov/34625399/

Freed, R. (2015). *Wired child: Reclaiming childhood in a digital age.* CreateSpace Independent Publishing Platform.

Freire, P. (1998). *Pedagogy of freedom: Ethics, democracy, and civic courage.* Rowman & Littlefield Publishers, Inc.

Freire, P., & Ramos, M. B. (1970). *Pedagogy of the oppressed.* Seabury Press.

French, S. A., Story, M., & Jeffery, R. W. (2001). Environmental influences on eating and physical activity. *Annual Review of Public Health, 22,* 309–335. https://doi.org/10.1146/annurev.publhealth.22.1.309

Gallup, Inc. (2017). *Time to play: A study on children's free time.* http://ww2.melissaanddoug.com/MelissaAndDoug_Gallup_TimetoPlay_Study.pdf

Gandini, L. (1993). Fundamentals of the Reggio Emilia approach to early childhood education. *Young Children, 49*(1), 4–8.

Goldstein, D. (2024, March 31). Watch these cute videos of babies (and learn something, too). *New York Times.* https://www.nytimes.com/2024/03/31/us/dan-wuori-child-development-videos.html

Gopnik, A., Meltzoff, A. N., & Kuhl, P. K. (1999). *The scientist in the crib: Minds, brains, and how children learn.* William Morrow.

Gottman, J. (1997). *Raising an emotionally intelligent child.* Simon & Schuster.

Grose, J. (2024, March 27). Screens are everywhere in schools. Do they actually help kids? *New York Times.* https://www.nytimes.com/2024/03/27/opinion/schools-technology.html

Grosshans, H. (2024). *Top 5 myths about kids' online safety legislation.* Common Sense Media. https://www.commonsensemedia.org/kids-action/articles/top-5-myths-about-kids-online-safety-legislation

Guernsey, L. (2007). *Into the minds of babes: How screen time affects children from birth to age five.* Basic Books.

Guernsey, L., Levine, M., Chiong, C., & Severns, M. (2012). *Pioneering literacy in the digital wild west: Empowering parents and educators.* Joan Ganz Cooney Center and New America Foundation. https://joanganzcooneycenter.org/wp-content /uploads/2012/12/GLR_TechnologyGuide_final.pdf

Hale, L., Kirschen, G. W., LeBourgeois, M. K., Gradisar, M., Garrison, M. M., Montgomery-Downs, H., Kirschen, H., McHale, S. M., Chang, A. M., & Buxton, O. M. (2018). Youth screen media habits and sleep: Sleep-friendly screen behavior recommendations for clinicians, educators, and parents. *Child and Adolescent Psychiatric Clinics of North America, 27*(2), 229–245. https://www.ncbi .nlm.nih.gov/pmc/articles/PMC5839336/

Harriman, N., Shortland, N., Su, M., Cote, T., Testa, M. A., & Savoia, E. (2020). Youth exposure to hate in the online space: An exploratory analysis. *International Journal of Environmental Research and Public Health, 17*(22), 8531. https://doi.org/10 .3390/ijerph17228531

Harrington, S. C., Stack, J., & O'Dwyer, V. (2019). Risk factors associated with myopia in schoolchildren in Ireland. *The British Journal of Ophthalmology, 103*(12), 1803–1809. https://doi.org/10.1136/bjophthalmol-2018-313325

Hartstein, L., Diniz, B., Wright, K., Akacem, L., Stowe, S., & LeBourgeois, M. (2023). Evening light intensity and phase delay of the circadian clock in early childhood. *Journal of Biological Rhythms, 38*(1), 77–86. https://doi.org/10.1177 /07487304221134330.

Heffler, K. F., Acharya, B., Subedi, K., & Bennett, D. S. (2024). Early-life digital media experiences and development of atypical sensory processing. *JAMA Pediatrics, 178*(3), 266–273. https://doi.org/10.1001/jamapediatrics.2023.5923

Heitner, D. (2023). *Growing up in public: Coming of age in a digital world.* Penguin Random House.

Herdzina, J., & Lauricella, A. R. (2020). *Media literacy in early childhood report: Framework, child development guidelines, and tips for implementation.* Erikson Institute Technology in Early Childhood Center. https://www.erikson.edu/wp-content /uploads/2021/06/TEC-MediaLiteracy-Report.pdf

Heubeck, E. (2024, January 15). Is too much screen time, too early, hindering reading comprehension? *Education Week Special Report.* https://www.edweek.org/tea ching-learning/is-too-much-screen-time-too-early-hindering-reading-com prehension/2024/01

Hiniker, A., Sobel, K., Suh, H., Sung, Y. C., Lee, C. P., & Kientz, J. A. (2015). Texting while parenting: How adults use mobile phones while caring for children at the playground. In B. Begole, J. Kim, K. Inkpen, & W. Woo (Eds.), *Proceedings of the 33rd ACM Conference on Human Factors in Computing Systems* (pp. 727–736). ACM. http://faculty.washington.edu/jkientz/papers/Hiniker-Texting-CHI2015.pdf

Hinkley, T., Verbestel, V., Ahrens, W., Lissner, L., Molnár, D., Moreno, L. A., Pigeot, I., Pohlabeln, H., Reisch, L. A., Russo, P., Veidebaum, T., Tornaritis, M., Williams, G., De Henauw, S., De Bourdeaudhuij, I., & IDEFICS Consortium (2014). Early childhood electronic media use as a predictor of poorer well-being: A prospective cohort study. *JAMA Pediatrics, 168*(5), 485–492. https://doi.org/10.1001/jamapediatrics.2014.94

Holden, B. A., Wilson, D. A., Jong, M., Sankaridurg, P., Fricke, T. R., Smith, E. L. III, & Resnikoff, S. (2015). Myopia: A growing global problem with sight-threatening complications. *Community Eye Health, 28*(90), 35.

Holmgren, H. G., Stockdale, L., Gale, M., & Coyne, S. M. (2022). Parent and child problematic media use: The role of maternal postpartum depression and dysfunctional parent-child interactions in young children. *Computers in Human Behavior, 133,* 107293. https://doi.org/10.1016/j.chb.2022.107293

Holohan, M. (2024, March). *Introducing the Screen Aware Early Childhood Action Kit: Tools and strategies for promoting healthy development in a screen-based world* [Conference presentation]. Vibrant Futures Champions for Child Care 50th Anniversary Summit, Grand Rapids, MI.

Holohan, M., Cantor, P., & Rogers, J. (2023, June 4–7). *Screen technologies change, children's developmental needs do not: Tools and strategies for prioritizing healthy development across learning environments* [Conference presentation]. National Association for the Education of Young Children Professional Learning Institute, Portland, OR.

Hooper, L., Livingstone, S., & Pothong, K. (2022). *Problems with data governance in UK schools: The cases of Google Classroom and ClassDojo.* Digital Futures Commission, 5Rights Foundation.

Hostinar, C. E., & Gunnar, M. R. (2015). Social support can buffer against stress and shape brain activity. *AJOB Neuroscience, 6*(3), 34–42. https://doi.org/10.1080/21507740.2015.1047054

Hutt, C. (1981). Toward a taxonomy and conceptual model of play. In H. K. Day (Ed.), *Advances in intrinsic motivation and aesthetics.* Springer. https://doi.org/10.1007/978-1-4613-3195-7_11

Hutton, J. S., Dudley, J., & Horowitz-Kraus, T. (2019). Associations between screen-based media use and brain white matter integrity in preschool-aged children. *JAMA Pediatrics, 174*(1), e193869. https://doi.org/10.1001/jamapediatrics.2019.3869

International Play Association. (2014). *Declaration on the importance of play.* http://ipaworld.org/ipa-declaration-on-the-importance-of-play/

Janssen, X., Martin, A., Hughes, A. R., Hill, C. M., Kotronouulas, G., & Hesketh, K. R. (2020). Associations of screen time, sedentary time and physical activity with sleep in under 5s: A systematic review and meta-analysis. *Sleep Medicine Review, 49,* 101226. https://doi.org/10.1016/j.smrv.2019.101226

Jolls, T., & Thoman, E. (2005). *Literacy for the 21st century: An overview and orientation guide to media literacy education.* Center for Media Literacy. http://www.medialit.org/sites/default/files/mlk/01_MLKorientation.pdf

Karani, N. F., Sher, J., & Mophosho, M. (2022). The influence of screen time on children's language development: A scoping review. *South African Journal of Communication Disorders, 69*(1), a825. https://doi.org/10.4102/sajcd.v69i1.825

Kirkorian, H. L., Pempek, T. A., Murphy, L. A., Schmidt, M. E., & Anderson, D. R. (2009). The impact of background television on parent-child interaction. *Child Development, 80*(5), 1350–1359.

Kourti, A., Stavridou, A., Panagouli, E., Psaltopoulou, T., Tsolia, M., Sergentanis, T. N., & Tsitsika, A. (2021). Play behaviors in children during the COVID-19 pandemic: A review of the literature. *Children, 8*, 706. https://doi.org/10.3390/children8080706

Krueger, A. (2024, June 9). Sign right here: The parents pledging to keep kids phone-free. *The New York Times.* https://www.nytimes.com/2024/06/09/style/sign-right-here-the-parents-pledging-to-keep-kids-phone-free.html?smid=nytcore-ios-share&referringSource=articleShare

Kumar, P. (February 4, 2019). *The real problem with posting about your kids online.* The Conversation. https://theconversation.com/the-real-problem-with-posting-about-your-kids-online-110131

Larouche, R., Garriguet, D., Gunnell, K. E., Goldfield, G. S., & Tremblay, M. S. (2016). *Outdoor time, physical activity, sedentary time, and health indicators at ages 7 to 14: 2012/2013 Canadian Health Measures Survey.* Statistics Canada. https://www150.statcan.gc.ca/n1/pub/82-003-x/2016009/article/14652-eng.htm

Law, E. C., Han, M. X., Lai, Z., Lim, S., Ong, Z. Y., Ng, V., Gabard-Durnam, L. J., Wilkinson, C. L., Levin, A. R., Rifkin-Graboi, A., Daniel, L. M., Gluckman, P. D., Chong, Y. S., Meaney, M. J., & Nelson, C. A. (2023). Associations between infant screen use, electroencephalography markers, and cognitive outcomes. *JAMA Pediatrics.* https://jamanetwork.com/journals/jamapediatrics/fullarticle/2800776

Leadbeater, B. J., Schellenbach, C. J., Maton, K. I., & Dodgen, D. W. (2004). Research and policy for building strengths: Processes and contexts of individual, family, and community development. In K. I. Maton, C. J. Schellenbach, B. J. Leadbeater, & A. L. Solarz (Eds.), *Investing in children, youth, families, and communities: Strengths-based research and policy* (1st ed., pp. 13–30). American Psychological Association.

Levin, D. (2013). *Beyond remote-controlled childhood: Teaching young children in the media age.* National Association for the Education of Young Children.

Levin, D., & Carlsson-Paige, N. (2006). *The war play dilemma.* Teachers College Press.

Levin, D., & Kilbourne, J. (2009) *So sexy, so soon.* Ballantine Books.

Lewin, T. (2009, October 23). No Einstein in your crib? Get a refund. *New York Times.* https://www.nytimes.com/2009/10/24/education/24baby.html

Li, C., Cheng, G., Sha, T., Cheng, W., & Yan, Y. (2020). The relationships between screen use and health indicators among infants, toddlers, and preschoolers: A meta-analysis and systematic review. *International Journal of Environmental Research and Public Health, 17*(19), 7324. https://doi.org/10.3390/ijerph17197324

Li, Q., Yu, Y., Wang, X., Wong, S. Y., & Yang, X. (2025). The relationship between parental affective disorders and digital addition in children and adolescents: A systematic review and meta-analysis. *Addictive Behaviors, 164*, 108282. https://doi.org/10.1016/j.addbeh.2025.108282

Linn, S. (2004). *Consuming kids: Protecting our children from the onslaught of marketing & advertising.* The New Press.

Linn, S. (2022). *Who's raising the kids? Big tech, big business, and the lives of children.* The New Press.

Liu, J., Ji, X., Pitt, S., Wang, G., Rovit, E., Lipman, T., & Jiang, F. (2024). Childhood sleep: Physical, cognitive, and behavioral consequences and implications. *World Journal of Pediatrics, 20*(2), 122–132. https://doi.org/10.1007/s12519-022-00647-w

Livingstone, S. (2016). Reframing media effects in terms of children's rights in the digital age. *Journal of Children and Media, 10*(1), 4–12. https://doi.org/10.1080/17482798.2015.1123164

Livingstone, S., & Blum-Ross, A. (2020). *Parenting for a digital future.* Oxford University Press.

Livingstone, S., & Stoilova, M. (2021). *The 4Cs: Classifying online risk to children.* (CO:RE Short Report Series on Key Topics). Hamburg: Leibniz-Institut für Medienforschung | Hans-Bredow-Institut (HBI); CO:RE Children Online: Research and Evidence. https://doi.org/10.21241/ssoar.71817

Louisiana Department of Health. (2024). *Louisiana screen time regulations toolkit for early childhood education centers.* Well-Ahead. https://wellaheadla.com/resource/louisiana-screen-time-regulations-toolkit-for-early-childhood-education-centers/

Madigan, S., McArthur, B. A., Anhorn, C., Eirich, R., & Christakis, D. A. (2020). Associations between screen use and child language skills: A systematic review and meta-analysis. *JAMA Pediatrics, 174*(7), 665–675. https://doi.org/10.1001/jamapediatrics.2020.0327

Mann, S., Calvin, A., Lenhart, A., & Robb, M. B. (2025). *The Common Sense census: Media use by kids zero to eight, 2025.* Common Sense Media. https://www.commonsensemedia.org/sites/default/files/research/report/2025-common-sense-census-web-2.pdf

Martinot, P., Bernard, J. Y., Peyre, H., DeAgostini, M., Forhan, A., Charles, M-A., Plancoulaine, S., & Heuded, B. (2021). Exposure to screens and children's language development in the EDEN mother-child cohort. *Scientific Reports, 11,* 11863. https://doi.org/10.1038/s41598-021-90867-3

Martzog, P., & Suggate, S. P. (2022). Screen media are associated with fine motor skill development in preschool children. *Early Childhood Research Quarterly, 60,* 363–373. https://doi.org/10.1016/j.ecresq.2022.03.010

Masterman, L. (1985). *Teaching the media* (1st ed.). Routledge. https://doi.org/10.4324/9780203359051

Maton, K. I., Dodgen, D. W., Leadbeater, B. J., Sandler, I. N., Schellenbach, C. J., & Solarz, A. L. (2004). Strengths-based research and policy: An introduction. In K. I. Maton, C. J. Schellenbach, B. J. Leadbeater, & A. L. Solarz (Eds.), *Investing in children, youth, families, and communities: Strengths-based research and policy* (1st ed., pp. 3–12). American Psychological Association.

McClelland, M., Tominey, S., Tracy, A., Nancarrow, A., & Karing, J. (2020). *Executive function in early childhood.* Education Hub. https://theeducationhub.org.nz/executive-function-in-early-childhood/

McCormick Center. (2014). *Technology usage in your early childhood program: Questions to consider.* McCormick Center for Early Childhood Leadership at National Louis

University. https://mccormickcenter.nl.edu/library/technology-usage-in-your-early-childhood-program-questions-to-consider/

McDaniel, B. T. (2019). Parent distraction with phones, reasons for use, and impacts on parenting and child outcomes: A review of the emerging research. *Human Behavior and Emerging Technologies, 1*(2), 72–80. https://doi.org/10.1002/hbe2.139

McDaniel, B. T., & Coyne, S. M. (2016). "Technoference": The interference of technology in couple relationships and implications for women's personal and relational well-being. *Psychology of Popular Media Culture, 5*(1), 85–98. https://doi.org/10.1037/ppm0000065

McDaniel, B. T., & Radesky, J. S. (2017). Technoference: Parent distraction with technology and associations with child behavior problems. *Child Development, 89*(1), 100–109. https://doi.org/10.1111/cdev.12822

McDaniel, B. T., & Radesky, J. S. (2018). Technoference: Longitudinal associations between parent technology use, parenting stress, and child behavior problems. *Pediatric Research, 84*, 210–218. https://doi.org/10.1038/s41390-018-0052-6

Mendelsohn, A. L., Berkule, S. B., Tomopoulos, S., Tamis-LeMonda, C. S., Huberman, H. S., Alvir, J., & Dreyer, B. P. (2008). Infant television and video exposure associated with limited parent-child verbal interactions in low socioeconomic status households. *Archives of Pediatric and Adolescent Medicine, 162*(5), 411–417.

Meyer, M., Adkins, V., Yuan, N., Weeks, H. M., Chang, Y-J., & Radesky, J. (2019, January). Advertising in young children's apps: A content analysis. *Journal of Developmental & Behavioral Pediatrics, 40*(1), 32–39. https://doi.org/10.1097/DBP.0000000000000622.

Mohan, A., Sen, P., Shah, C., Jain, E., & Jain, S. (2021). Prevalence and risk factor assessment of digital eye strain among children using online e-learning during the COVID-19 pandemic: Digital eye strain among kids (DESK study-1). *Indian Journal of Ophthalmology, 69*(1), 140–144. https://doi.org/10.4103/ijo.IJO_2535_20.

Morawska, A., Mitchell, A. E., & Tooth, L. R. (2023). Managing screen use in the under-fives: Recommendations for parenting intervention development. *Clinical Child and Family Psychology Review, 26*, 943–956. https://doi.org/10.1007/s10567-023-00435-6

Myers, L. J., Crawford, E., Murphy, C., Aka-Ezoua, E., & Felix, C. (2018). Eyes in the room trump eyes on the screen: Effects of a responsive co-viewer on toddlers' responses to and learning from video chat. *Journal of Children and Media, 12*(3), 275–294. https://doi.org/10.1080/17482798.2018.1425889

Myruski, S., Gulyayeva, O., Birk, S., Pérez-Edgar, K., Buss, K. A., & Dennis-Tiwary, T. A. (2018). Digital disruption? Maternal mobile device use is related to infant social-emotional functioning. *Developmental Science, 21*(4), e12610. https://doi.org/10.1111/desc.12610.

National Association for the Education of Young Children. (n.d.). *Principles of effective family engagement.* https://www.naeyc.org/resources/topics/family-engagement/principles

National Association for the Education of Young Children & Fred Rogers Center for Early Learning and Children's Media. (2012). *Technology and interactive media as tools in early childhood programs serving children from birth through age 8.* https://www.naeyc.org/sites/default/files/globally-shared/downloads/PDFs/resources/position-statements/ps_technology.pdf

National Association for Media Literacy Education. (n.d.). *Media Literacy definition.* https://namle.org/resources/media-literacy-defined/

National Center on Teaching and Learning. (n.d.). *The inquiry cycle.* Early Childhood National Centers. https://eclkc.ohs.acf.hhs.gov/sites/default/files/pdf/no-search/iss/steam/op-handout-2-tips-education-staff-inquiry-cycle.pdf

National Digital Inclusion Alliance (n.d.). *Definitions.* https://www.digitalinclusion.org/definitions/

National Scientific Council on the Developing Child. (2015). *Supportive relationships and active skill-building strengthen the foundations of resilience: Working Paper 13.* https://developingchild.harvard.edu/wp-content/uploads/2015/05/The-Science-of-Resilience.pdf

Nature. (2017). The digital native is a myth. *Nature, 547,* 380. https://doi.org/10.1038/547380a

Navarro, J. L., & Tudge, J. R. H. (2022).Technologizing Bronfenbrenner: Neo-ecological theory. *Current Psychology, 42,* 19338–19354. https://doi.org/10.1007/s12144-022-02738-3

Nelson, L. (2016, May 11). *Worrying over kids playing with phones and tablets is just another way to shame mothers.* Vox. https://www.vox.com/2016/5/11/11607544/screen-time-kids-parents-feminism

New York State Division of Child Care Services. (2021). *Child care regulations, child day care centers.* https://ocfs.ny.gov/programs/childcare/regulations/

Nichols, D. L. (2022). The context of background TV exposure and children's executive functioning. *Pediatric Research, 92,* 1168–1174. https://doi.org/10.1038/s41390-021-01916-6

Nightingale, C. M., Rudnicka, A. R., Donin, A. S., Sattar, N., Cook, D. G., Whincup, P. H., & Owen, C. G. (2017). Screen time is associated with adiposity and insulin resistance in children. *Archives of Disease in Childhood, 102*(7), 612–616. https://doi.org/10.1136/archdischild-2016-312016

Nomkin, L. G., & Gordon, I. (2021). The relationship between maternal smartphone use, physiological responses, and gaze patterns during breastfeeding and face-to-face interactions with infant. *PloS One, 16*(10), e0257956. https://doi.org/10.1371/journal.pone.0257956

North, A. (2023, June 20). *The decline of American playtime—and how to resurrect it.* Vox. https://www.vox.com/23759898/kids-children-parenting-play-anxiety-mental-health

O'Toole, K. J., & Kannass, K. N. (2021). Background television and distractibility in young children: Does program content matter? *Journal of Applied Developmental Psychology, 75,* 101280. https://doi.org/10.1016/j.appdev.2021.101280

OECD. (2024). *Towards digital safety by design for children.* (OECD Digital Economy Papers, No. 363). OECD Publishing. https://doi.org/10.1787/c167b650-en

Outdoor Play Canada. (2015). *Position statement on active outdoor play.* https://www
.outdoorplaycanada.ca/wp-content/uploads/2019/07/position-statement-on
-active-outdoor-play-en.pdf

Parent Coalition for Student Privacy & Badass Teachers Association. (2018). *Educator toolkit for teacher and student privacy: A practical guide for protecting personal data.* https://studentprivacymatters.org/educator-toolkit-for-teacher-and-student
-privacy/

Pattoni, L. (2012). *Strengths-based approaches for working with individuals* (Insights: Evidence-based summaries to support social services in Scotland, 16). Institute for Research and Innovation in Social Services. https://www.iriss.org.uk
/resources/insights/strengths-based-approaches-working-individuals

Paul, C. D., Hansen, S. G., Marelle, C., & Wright, M. (2023). Incorporating technology into instruction in early childhood classrooms: A systematic review. *Advances in Neurodevelopmental Disorders, 7,* 380–391. https://doi.org/10.1007
/s41252-023-00316-7

Pauze, E., & Kent, M. P. (2021). Children's measured exposure to food and beverage advertising on television in Toronto. *Canadian Journal of Public Health, 112*(6), 1008–1019 https://doi.org/10.17269/s41997-021-00528-1.

Pica, R. (2024). *The earlier the better? Pushing academics on young children is counterproductive.* Community Playthings. https://www.communityplaythings.com/resources
/articles/the-earlier-the-better

Pila, S., Blackwell, C. K., Lauricella, A. R., & Wartella, E. (2019). *Technology in the lives of educators and early childhood programs: 2018 survey.* Center on Media and Human Development, Northwestern University. https://cmhd.northwestern
.edu/wp-content/uploads/2019/08/NAEYC-Report-2019.pdf

Plowman, L. (2020). *Digital play.* Centre for Research in Digital Education, University of Edinburgh. https://www.de.ed.ac.uk/sites/default/files/2020-07/Digital
%20Play%20-%20Plowman%202020.pdf

Ponti, M. (2023). *Position Statement: Screen time and preschool children: Promoting health and development in a digital world. Paediatrics & Child Health, 28*(3), 184–192. https://cps.ca/en/documents/position/screen-time-and-preschool-children

Prensky, M. (2001). Digital natives, digital immigrants. *On the Horizon, 9(5),* 1–6. (MCB University Press). https://marcprensky.com/writing/Prensky%20-%20
Digital%20Natives,%20Digital%20Immigrants%20-%20Part1.pdf

Puglisi, D. (n.d.). *"In child development, conversation is the golden nugget": A conversation with Kathy Hirsh-Pasek.* First Things First. https://www.firstthingsfirst.org/first
-things/child-development-conversation-golden-nugget-2/

Radesky, J., Hiniker, A., & McLaren, C. (2022). Prevalence and characteristics of manipulative design in mobile applications used by children. *JAMA Network Open, 5*(6), e2217641. https://jamanetwork.com/journals/jamanetworkopen
/fullarticle/2793493

Radesky, J. S., Kistin, C. J., Zuckerman, B., Nitzberg, K., Gross, J., Kaplan-Sanoff, M., Augustyn, M., & Silverstein, M. (2014). Patterns of mobile device use by caregivers and children during meals in fast food restaurants. *Pediatrics, 133*(4), e843–e849. https://doi.org/10.1542/peds.2013-3703

Radesky, J. S., Peacock-Chambers, E., Zuckerman, B., & Silverstein, M. (2016). Use of mobile technology to calm upset children: Associations with social-emotional development. *JAMA Pediatrics, 170*(4), 397–399. https://doi.org/10.1001/jamapediatrics.2015.4260

Raney, M. A., Daniel, E., & Jack, N. (2023). Impact of urban school yard play zone diversity and nature-based design features on unstructured recess play behaviors. *Landscape and Urban Planning,* 230, 104632. https://doi.org/10.1016/j.landurbplan.2022.104632

Rega, V., Gioia, F., & Boursier, V. (2023). Problematic media use among children up to the age of 10: A systematic literature review. *International Journal of Environmental Research and Public Health, 20*(10), 5854. https://doi.org/10.3390/ijerph20105854

Ribner, A. D., McHarg, G. G., & NewFAMS Study Team. (2019). Why won't she sleep? Screen exposure and sleep patterns in young infants. *Infant Behavior & Development,* 57, 101334. https://doi.org/10.1016/j.infbeh.2019.101334

Rideout, V., & Robb, M. B. (2020). *The Common Sense census: Media use by kids age zero to eight, 2020.* Common Sense Media. https://www.commonsensemedia.org/sites/default/files/research/report/2020_zero_to_eight_census_final_web.pdf

Rix, K. (2022, October 14). How much recess should kids get? *U.S. News and World Report.* https://www.usnews.com/education/k12/articles/how-much-recess-should-kids-get

Robinson, C. A., Domoff, S. E., Kasper, N., Peterson, K. E., & Miller, A. L. (2022). The healthfulness of children's meals when multiple media and devices are present. *Appetite, 169,* 105800. https://doi.org/10.1016/j.appet.2021.105800

Robinson, L., Smith, M., Segal, J., & Shubin, J. (2024). *The benefits of play for adults.* HelpGuide.org. https://www.helpguide.org/articles/mental-health/benefits-of-play-for-adults.htm

Robinson, T. N., Banda, J. A., Hale, L., Lu, A. S., Fleming-Milici, F., Calvert, S. L., & Wartella, E. (2017). Screen media exposure and obesity in children and adolescents. *Pediatrics, 140*(Suppl 2), S97–S101. https://doi.org/10.1542/peds.2016-1758K

Rogow, F. (2022). *Media literacy for young children: Teaching beyond the screen time debates.* National Association for the Education of Young Children.

Rogow, F. (2023). Framing: How we think about our work. *Young Children,* 78(4), 6–14.

Rosanbalm, K.D., & Murray, D.W. (2017). *Caregiver co-regulation across development: A practice brief* (OPRE Brief #2017–80). Office of Planning, Research, and Evaluation, Administration for Children and Families, U.S. Department of Health and Human Services. https://www.acf.hhs.gov/opre/report/co-regulation-birth-through-young-adulthood-practice-brief

Rovee-Collier, C., & Gekoski, S. S. (1972). The contribution of the infant's own activity to its development of a sense of causality. *Developmental Psychology,* 6(1), 109–118.

Samuelsson, R., Price, S., & Jewitt, C. (2022). How young children's play is shaped through common iPad applications: A study of 2- and 4–5-year-olds. *Learning, Media, and Technology, 49*(2), 151–169. https://doi.org/10.1080/17439884.2022.2141252

Saner, E. (2018, May 24). The 'sharent' trap: Should you ever put your children on social media? *The Guardian.* https://www.theguardian.com/lifeandstyle/2018/may/24/sharent-trap-should-parents-put-their-children-on-social-media-instagram

Santos, R. M. S., Mendes, C. G., Miranda, D. M., & Romano-Silva, M. A. (2022). The association between screen time and attention in children: A systematic review. *Developmental Neuropsychology, 47*(4), 175–192. https://doi.org/10.1080/87565641.2022.2064863.

Scales, P. C., Benson, P. L., Oesterle, S., Hill, K. G., Hawkins, J. D., & Pashak, T. J. (2015). The dimensions of successful young adult development: A conceptual and measurement framework. *Applied Developmental Science, 20*(3), 150–174. https://doi.org/10.1080/10888691.2015.1082429

Share, J. (2015). *Media literacy is elementary: Teaching youth to critically read and create media* (2nd ed.). Peter Lang Publishing.

Shawcroft, J., Blake, H., Gonzalez, A., & Coyne, S. M. (2023). Structures for screens: Longitudinal associations between parental media rules and problematic media use in early childhood. *Technology, Mind, and Behavior, 4*(2), tmb0000104. https://tmb.apaopen.org/pub/pr7c69im/release/1

Shin, W. (2018). Empowered parents: The role of self-efficacy in parental mediation of children's smartphone use in the United States. *Journal of Children and Media, 12*(4), 465–477. https://doi.org/10.1080/17482798.2018.1486331

Shinde, Y. (2024). *K–12 education technology spend market grow USD 132.4 bn by 2034.* Market.us.scoop. https://scoop.market.us/k-12-education-technology-spend-market-grow-usd-132-4-bn-by-2032/.

Siibak, A., & Mascheroni, G. (2021). *Children's data and privacy in the digital age* (CO:RE Short Report Series on Key Topics). Leibniz-Institut für Medienforschung | Hans-Bredow-Institut (HBI); CO:RE—Children Online: Research and Evidence. https://doi.org/10.21241/ssoar.76251

Singer, N. (2024, August 11). The school tech problem. *New York Times.* https://www.nytimes.com/2024/08/11/briefing/techonology-schools.html

Smith, D. (2024, April 2). How exercise strengthens your brain. *New York Times.* https://www.nytimes.com/2024/04/02/well/mind/exercise-mental-health-cognition.html

Snider, K. A., Adams, A., Petet, N., Birk, S., & Tittle, B. (2023). Take me to the movies! Using digital play and project work to spark young children's inquiry and learning. *Young Children, 78*(4), 22–29.

Staiano, A. E., Allen, A. T., Fowler, W., Gustat, J., Kepper, M. M., Lewis, L., Martin, C. K., St. Romain, J., & Webster, E. K. (2018). State licensing regulations on screen time in childcare centers: An impetus for participatory action research. *Progress in Community Health Partnerships: Research, Education, and Action, 12,* 101–109. https://doi.org/10.1353/cpr.2018.0025

Strouse, G. A., & Ganea, P. A. (2016). Are prompts provided by electronic books as effective for teaching preschoolers a biological concept as those provided by adults? *Early Education and Development, 27,* 1190–1204. https://doi.org/10.1080/10409289.2016.1210457

Swartz, M. I., Bartlett, J. D., & Vele-Tabaddor, E. (2016). Strengths-based education and practices. In D. L. Couchenour & K. Chrisman (Eds.), *The SAGE encyclopedia of contemporary early childhood education* (pp. 1301–1304). SAGE Publications, Inc.

Swit, C. S., Coyne, S. M., Shawcroft, J., Garth, M., Barr, R., Holmgren, H. G., & Stockdale, L. (2023). Problematic media use in early childhood: The role of parent-child relationships and parental wellbeing in families in New Zealand and the United States. *Journal of Children and Media, 17*(4), 443–466. https://doi.org/10.1080/17482798.2023.2230321

Takahashi, I., Obara, T., Ishikuro M., Murakami, K., Ueno, F., Noda, A., Onuma, T., Shinoda, G., Nishimura, T., Tsuchiya, K. J., & Kuriyama, S. (2023). Screen time at age 1 year and communication and problem-solving developmental delay at 2 and 4 years. *JAMA Pediatrics, 177*(10), 1039–1046. https://doi.org/10.1001/jamapediatrics.2023.3057

Teichert, L. (2017). To digital or not to digital: How mothers are navigating the digital world with their young children. *Language and Literacy, 19*(1), 63–76.

Thompson, P. (2017). Cognitive development: The theory of Jean Piaget. Foundations of educational technology. https://open.library.okstate.edu/foundationsofeducationaltechnology/chapter/2-cognitive-development-the-theory-of-jean-piaget/

Tremblay, M. S., Gray, C., Babcock, S., Barnes, J., Bradstreet, C. C., Carr, D., Chabot, G., Choquette, L., Chorney, D., Collyer, C., Herrington, S., Janson, K., Janssen, I., Larouche, R., Pickett, W., Power, M., Sandseter, E. B., Simon, B., & Brussoni, M. (2015). Position statement on active outdoor play. *International Journal of Environmental Research and Public Health, 12*(6), 6475–6505. https://doi.org/10.3390/ijerph120606475

Tronick, E., Als, H., Adamson, L., Wise, S., & Brazelton, T. B. (1978). The infant's response to entrapment between contradictory messages in face-to-face interaction. *Journal of the American Academy of Child Psychiatry, 17*(1), 1–13. https://doi.org/10.1016/s0002-7138(09)62273-1

Undheim, M. (2022). Children and teachers engaging together with digital technology in early childhood education and care institutions: A literature review. *European Early Childhood Education Research Journal, 30*(3), 472–489. https://doi.org/10.1080/1350293X.2021.1971730

UNICEF. (2024). *Digital technology, play and child well-being report.* Responsible Innovation in Technology for Children. UNICEF Innocenti Global Office of Research and Foresight. https://www.unicef.org/innocenti/media/8056/file/UNICEF-Innocenti-RITEC-P2-report-2024.pdf.pdf

United Nations Convention on the Rights of the Child, November 20, 1989. https://www.unicef.org/child-rights-convention

Vanden Abeele, M. M., Abels, M., & Hendrickson, A. T. (2020). Are parents less responsive to young children when they are on their phones? A systematic naturalistic observation study. *Cyberpsychology, Behavior, and Social Networking, 23*(6), 363–370. https://doi.org/10.1089/cyber.2019.0472

Vygotsky, L. S. (1978). *Mind in society: The development of higher psychological processes.* Harvard University Press.

Walker, S. K. (2022). *Critical perspectives on technology and the family.* University of Minnesota Libraries Publishing.

Wells, N. M., & Evans, G. W. (2003). Nearby nature: A buffer of life stress among rural children. *Environment and Behavior, 35*(3): 311–330. https://doi.org/10.1177/0013916503035003001.

Willcott, J. (2017, February 11). *How EdTech companies are getting a foothold in the classroom.* EdSurge. https://www.edsurge.com/news/2017-02-11-how-edtech-companies-are-getting-a-foothold-in-the-classroom

World Health Organization. (2019). *Guidelines on physical activity, sedentary behaviour, and sleep for children under 5 years of age.* Author. https://www.who.int/publications/i/item/9789241550536

World Health Organization. (2020). *WHO guidelines on physical activity and sedentary behaviour: Executive summary.* Author. https://www.ncbi.nlm.nih.gov/books/NBK566048/

Yang, G. Y., Huang, L. H., Schmid, K. L., Li, C. G., Chen, J. Y., He, G. H., Liu, L., Ruan, Z. L., & Chen, W. Q. (2020). Associations between screen exposure in early life and myopia amongst Chinese preschoolers. *International Journal of Environmental Research and Public Health, 17*(3), 1056. https://doi.org/10.3390/ijerph17031056

Yogman, M., Garner, A., Hutchinson, J., Hirsh-Pasek, K., & Golinkoff, R. M. (2018). AAP Council on Communications and Media. The power of play: A pediatric role in enhancing development in young children. *Pediatrics, 142*(3), e20182058. https://doi.org/10.1542/peds.2018-2058

Zack, E., & Barr, R. (2016). The role of interactional quality in learning from touch screens during infancy: Context matters. *Frontiers in Psychology, 7*, 210408. https://doi.org/10.3389/fpsyg.2016.01264

Zosh, J. M., Hirsh-Pasek, K., Hopkins, E. J., Jensen, H., Liu, C., Neale, D., Solis, S. L., & Whitebread, D. (2018). Accessing the inaccessible: Redefining play as a spectrum. *Frontiers in Psychology, 9*, 1124. https://doi.org/10.3389/fpsyg.2018.01124

Index

About the Authors

Patricia Cantor is Professor Emerita of Early Childhood Studies and former Associate Provost at Plymouth State University, New Hampshire. She is co-author of the book *Techwise Infant and Toddler Teachers: Making Sense of Screen Media for Children Under 3*, which has introduced many educators to technology and marketing issues that impact young children. A former preschool teacher and child care center director, Pat has inspired a generation of educators and practitioners to understand and appreciate the critical importance of child development, teaching courses in play, inclusive early education, infant and toddler care and education, the history and philosophy of early childhood education, and early childhood advocacy and policy. She co-authored the *New Hampshire Early Learning Standards for Children Birth Through Age 5* and has published articles in early childhood journals. Pat is the recipient of awards for excellence in teaching, distinguished educational leadership, professional service, and promoting excellence in early learning through teacher professional development.

Melinda Holohan is a faculty member in Family Science and Human Development at Western Michigan University, specializing in the critical intersection of early childhood development, family systems, and digital media. She applies a constructivist approach, and extensive experience in childcare, early learning, and professional development, to her work with college students and child, youth, and family studies programs. Mindy is a National Council on Family Relations' Certified Family Life Educator and frequently invited presenter and workshop leader, providing actionable strategies for understanding and promoting child and family well-being in the digital age. Recognizing growing challenges for families and practitioners, she co-founded the Early Childhood Work Group at the Screen Time Action Network, where she led the creation of the Screen Aware Early Childhood Action Kit and continues to support members in their advocacy efforts.

Jean Rogers is director of the Screen Time Action Network at Fairplay, a global collaborative of practitioners, educators, advocates, and parents working to reduce excessive and harmful screen use in childhood and keep kids safe online. She is an expert in designing national and international programs, movement-building, and establishing key partnerships that support child well-being in a digital world. Her NextGen Connect program is an intergenerational incubator that empowers young people—the generation experiencing the harms of digital socialization—to create solutions for their peers and generations to come. She is the author of *Kids Under Fire: Seven Simple Steps to Combat the Media Attack on Your Child*, a parenting guide that helps parents empower children to make healthy media choices. Jean is a Certified Parent Educator, specializing in how screen media impacts family life and child development, and a Certified Digital Wellness Educator who was named one of 12 thought leaders in the field in the *Digital Wellness Collaborative Report 2020.*